Authentic
GUITAR-TAB
Edition ™
Includes Complete Solos

James Taylor: GREATEST HITS

CONTENTS

Key To Notation Symbols

Something in the way she moves

Words and Music by
JAMES TAYLOR

*Capo at 3rd fret. The number 3 in tab represents a capoed open string.

that seems_ to leave_ this trou-bled world be-hind.

Substitute Fill 1 on D.S.

If I'm feel-in' down. an' blue_

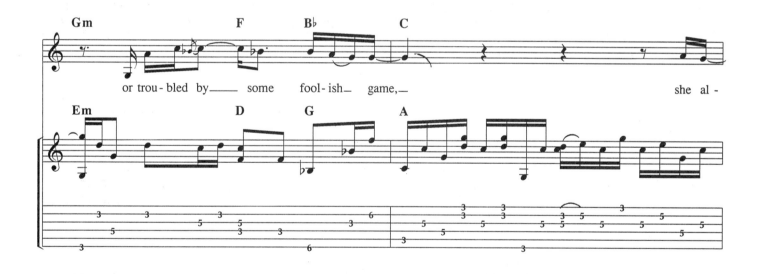

or trou-bled by__ some fool-ish_ game,_ she al-

Fill 1

8

ways seems_ to make me change_ my mind.___ (An') I feel___

Chorus:

fine an-y time___ she's a-round_ me now.___ She's a-round_

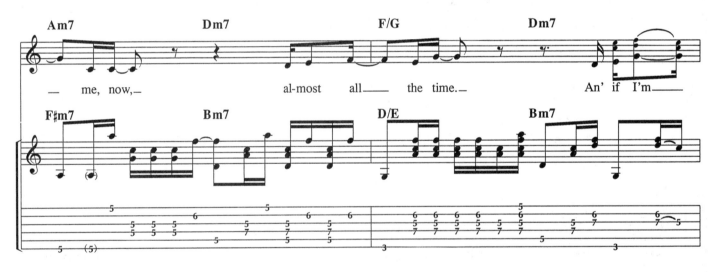

— me, now,— al-most all___ the time.— An' if I'm___

well you can tell_ that she's_ been with_ me now. She's been with.

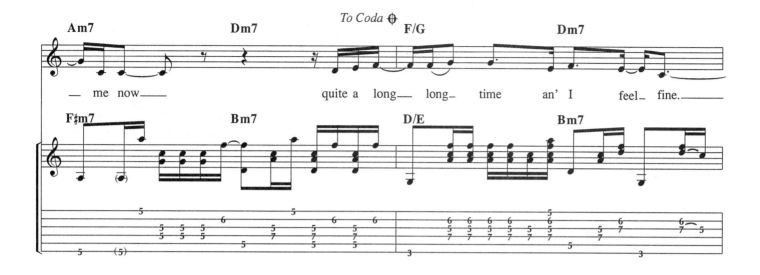

— me now___   quite a long___ long___ time an' I   feel___ fine.___

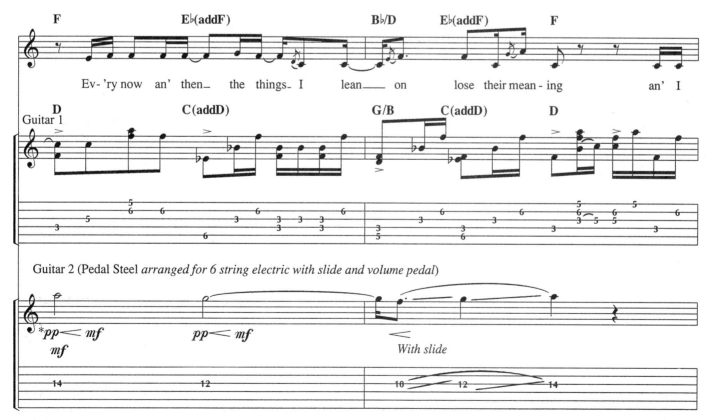

Ev-'ry now an' then___ the things___ I lean___ on   lose their mean-ing   an' I

Guitar 1

Guitar 2 (Pedal Steel *arranged for 6 string electric with slide and volume pedal*)

pp < *mf*   *pp* < *mf*

mf   *With slide*

*Fast volume swells

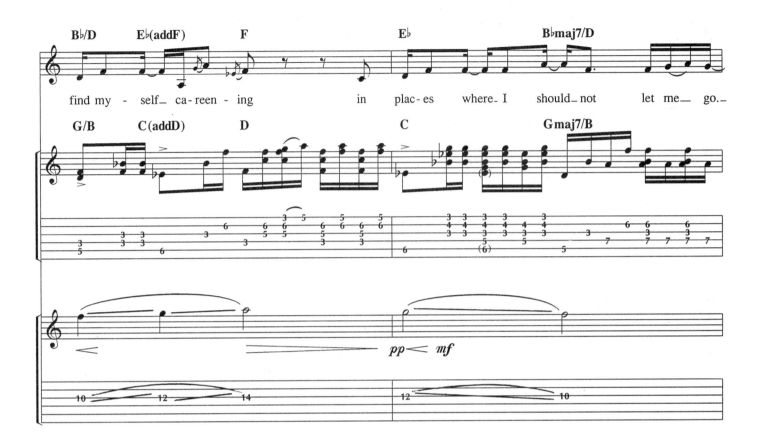

find my - self ca - reen - ing in plac - es where I should not let me go.

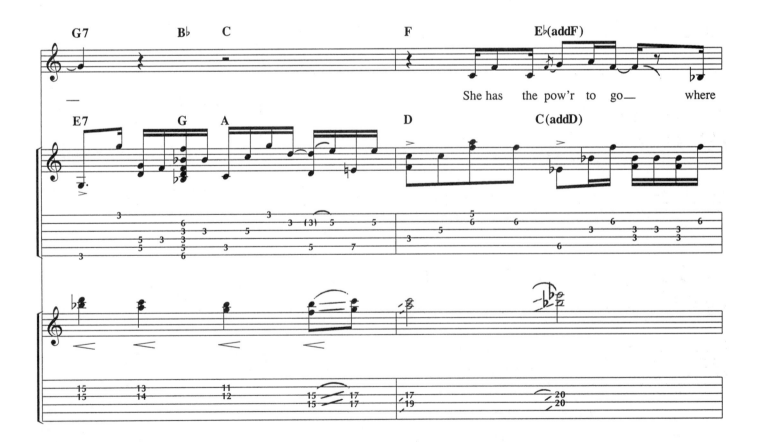

She has the pow'r to go where

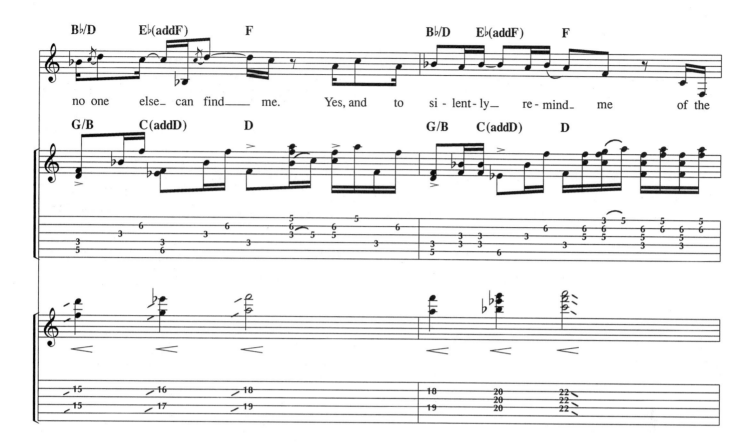

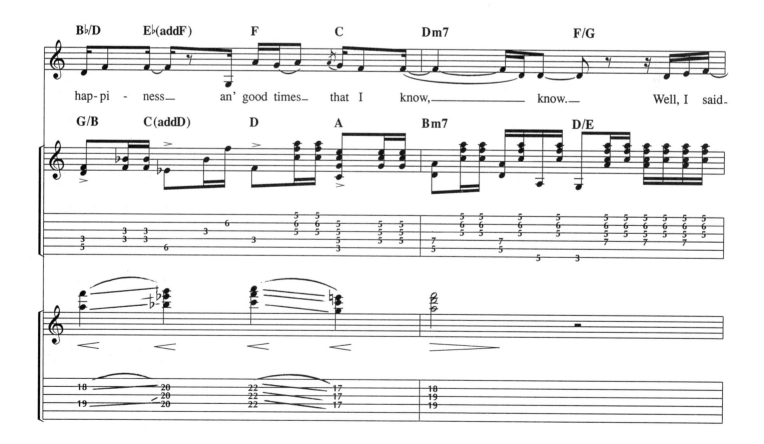

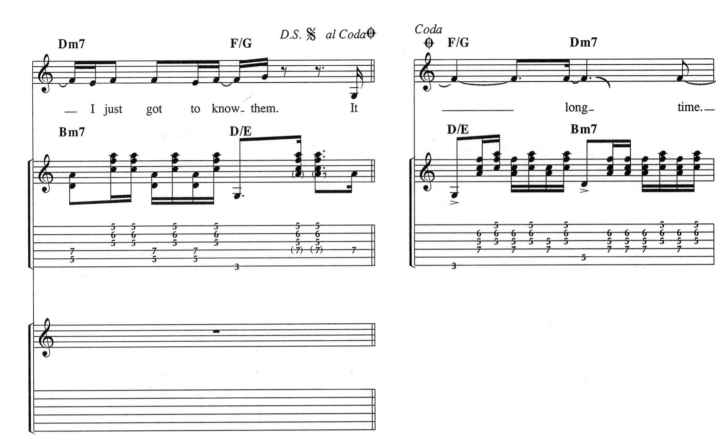

Additional Lyrics

Verse 2: It isn't what she's got to say,
Or how she thinks or where she's been.
To me, the words are nice the way they sound.
I like to hear them best that way.
It doesn't much matter what they mean,
Well, she says them mostly just to calm me down.
And I feel . . .

Carolina in my mind

Words and Music by
JAMES TAYLOR

*Capo at 2nd fret.

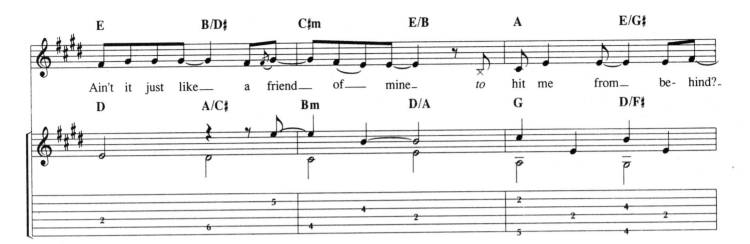

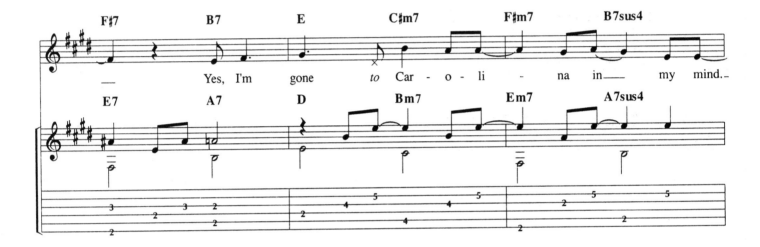

Watch her watch the morn-ing come.

*Arranged for Guitar

sil - ver tear__ ap - pear - ing__ now__ I'm__ cry - ing, ain't I? *I'm*

gone to Car - o - li - na in _ my mind. _

Pedal steel tacet

There

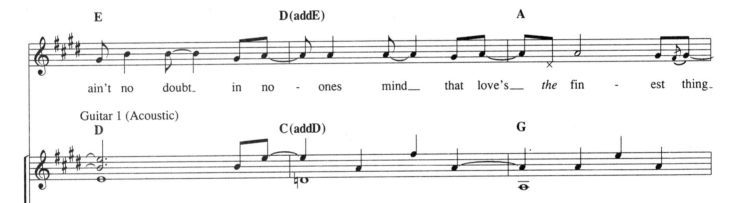

E   D(addE)   A

ain't no doubt _ in no - ones mind _ that love's _ *the* fin - est thing _

Guitar 1 (Acoustic)

D   C(addD)   G

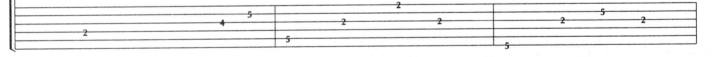

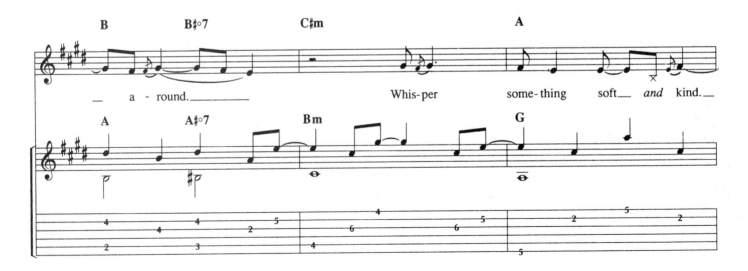

B   B#°7   C#m   A

_ a - round. _   Whis-per some-thing soft _ *and* kind. _

A   A#°7   Bm   G

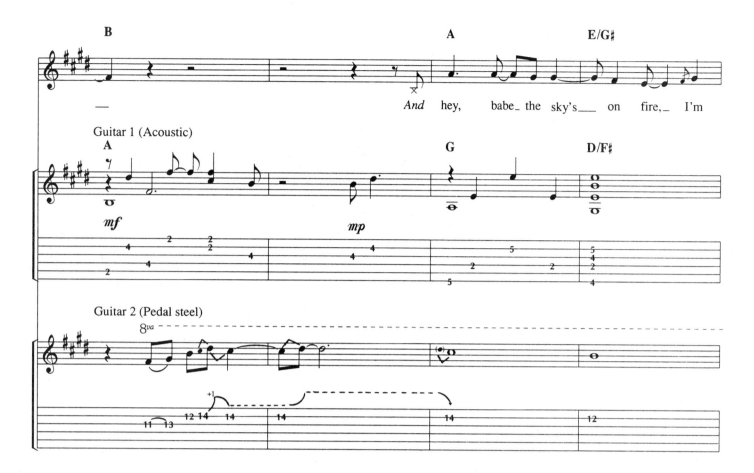

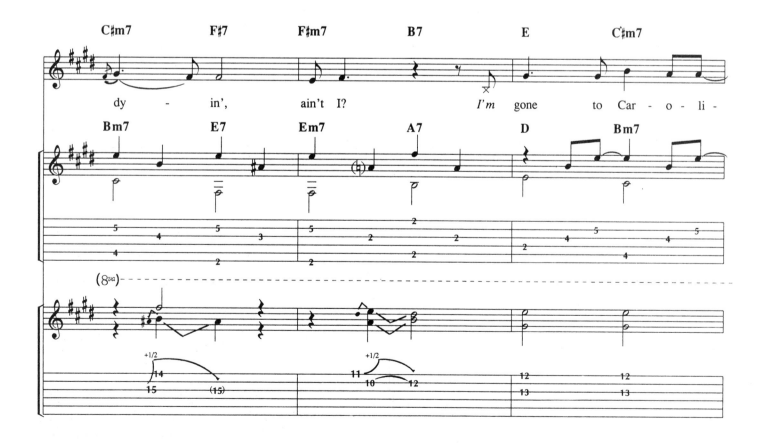

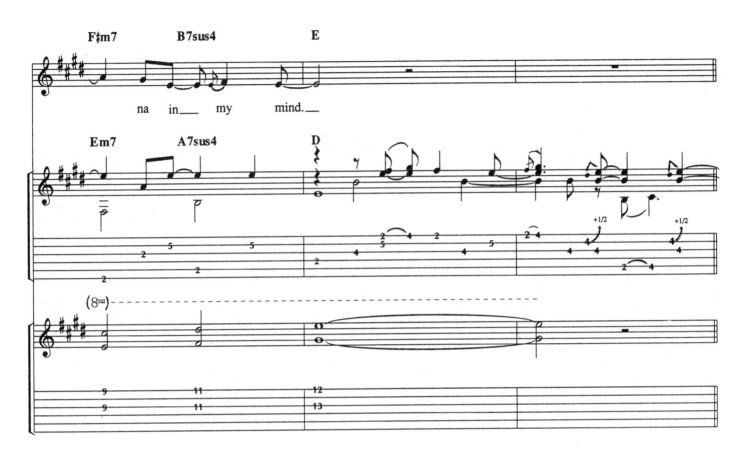

na in___ my mind.___

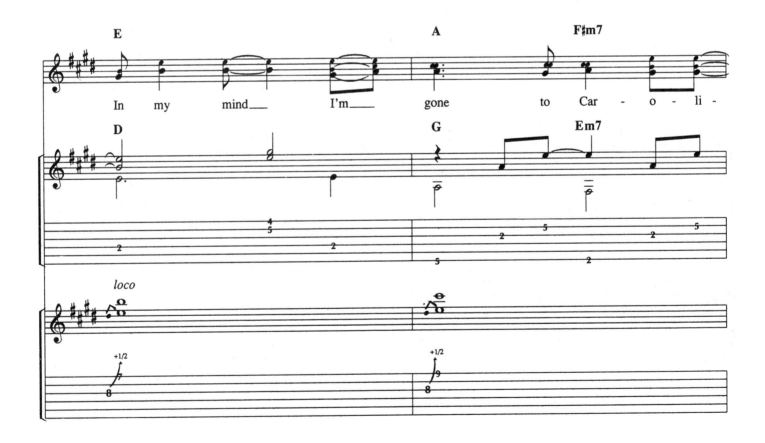

In my mind___ I'm___ gone to Car - o - li-

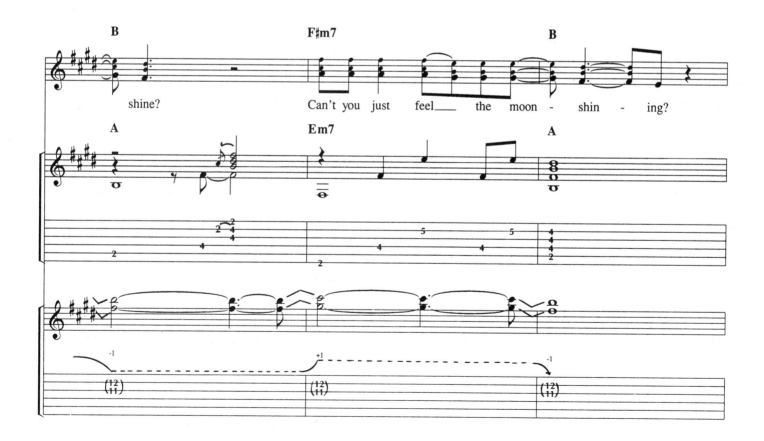

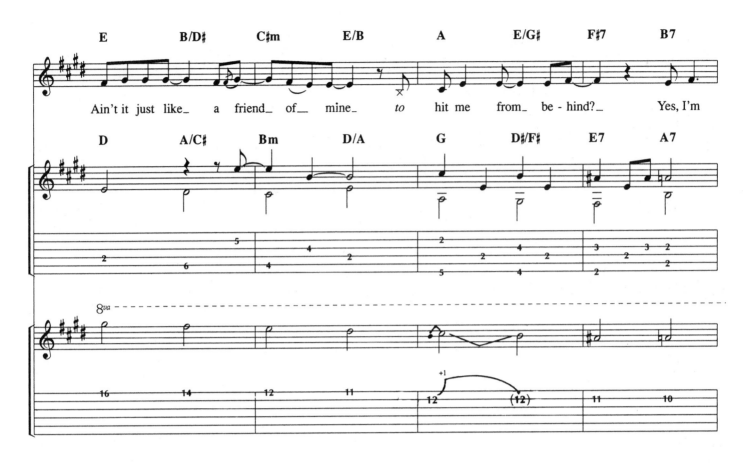

Ain't it just like_ a friend_ of_ mine_ *to* hit me from_ be - hind?_ Yes, I'm

gone to Car - o - li - na in_ my mind._

_ me, still I'm on_ the dark_ side of_ the moon._

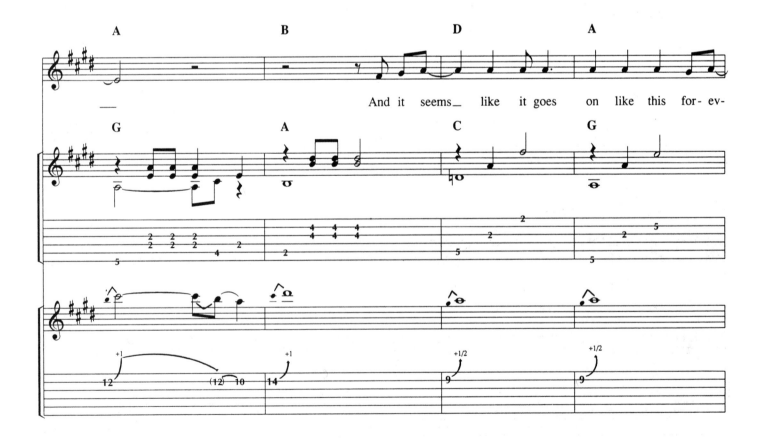

And it seems_ like it goes on like this for-ev-

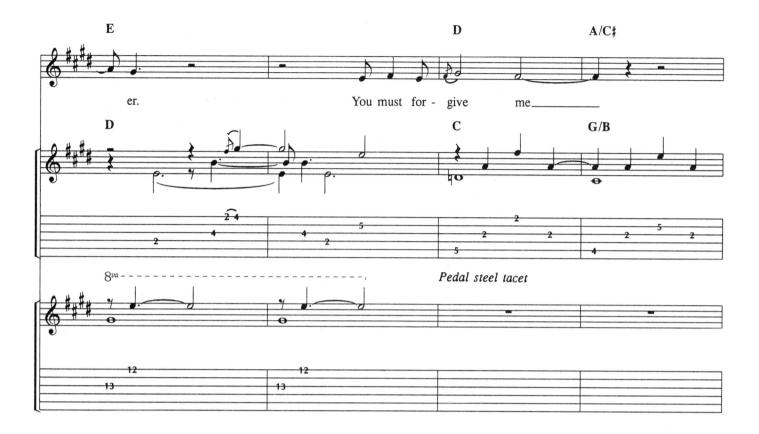

er. You must for - give me_____

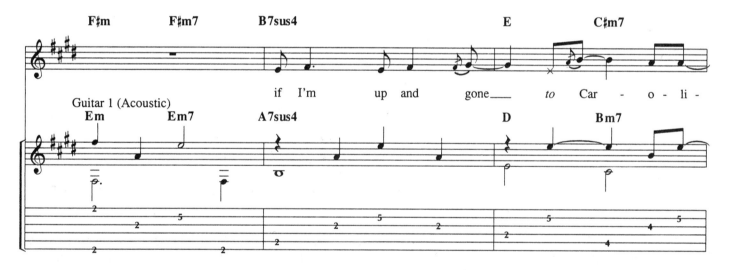

Guitar 1 (Acoustic)

if I'm up and gone___ *to* Car - o - li -

na in___ my mind.___

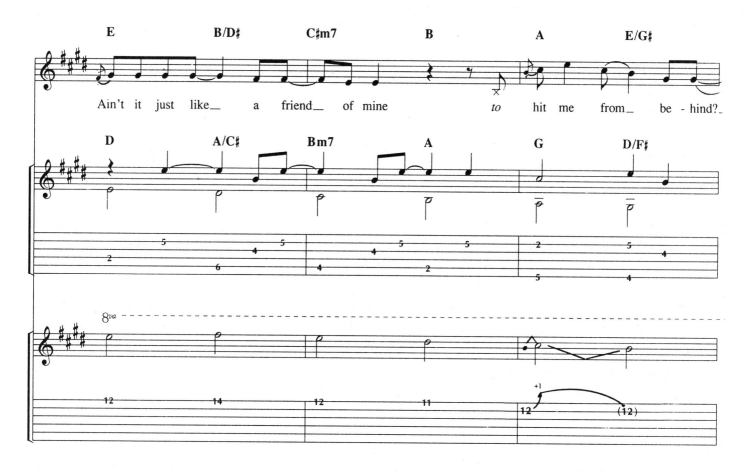

Ain't it just like_ a friend_ of mine *to* hit me from_ be - hind?_

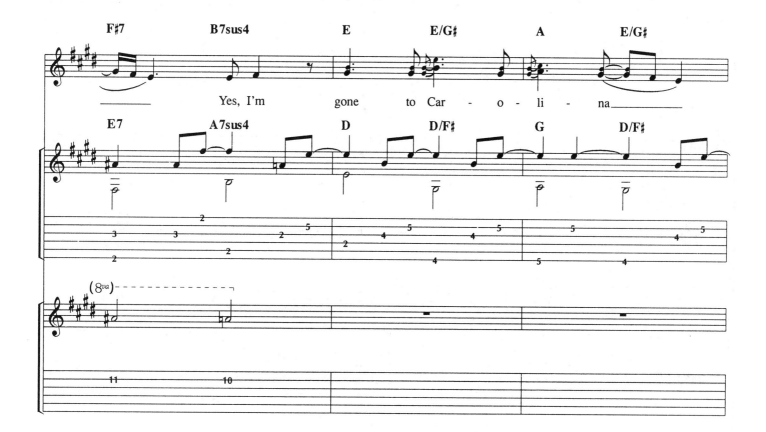

_ Yes, I'm gone to Car - o - li - na_____

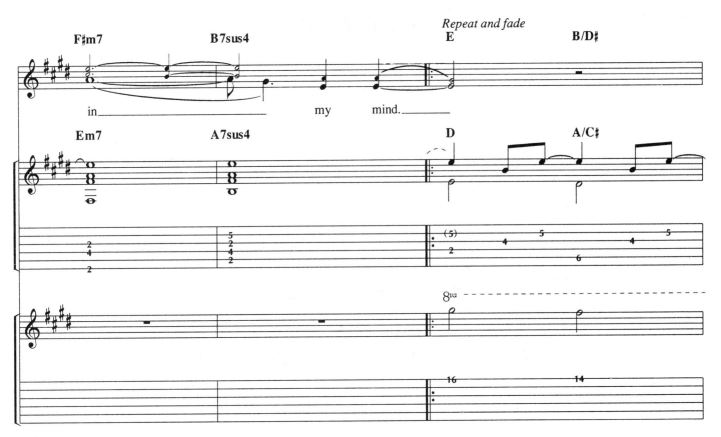

Repeat and fade

in_____ my mind._____

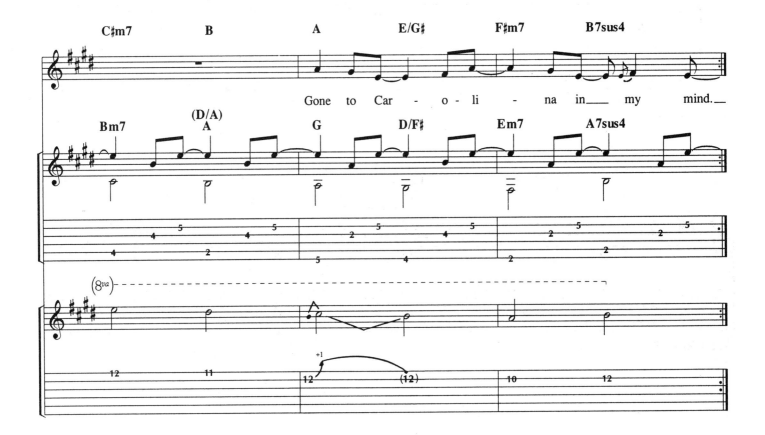

Gone to Car - o - li - na in___ my mind.__

Fire and rain

Words and Music by
JAMES TAYLOR

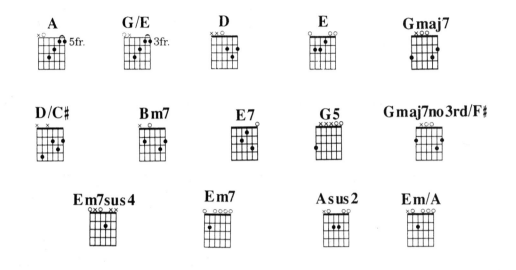

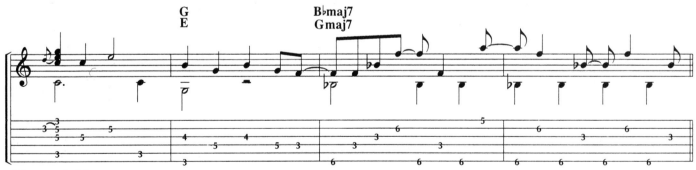

*Capo at 3rd fret.

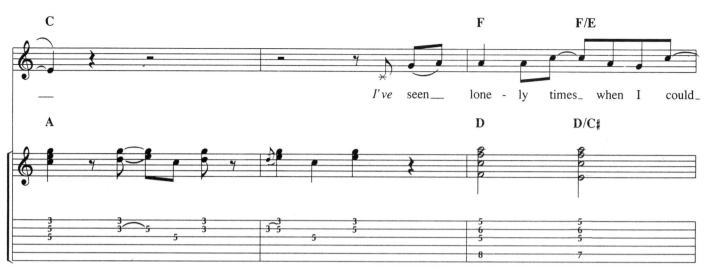

C   **F**   **F/E**

_I've_ seen__ lone - ly times__ when I could__

A   **D**   **D/C♯**

Dm7   **G7**   **C**   _With Fill 2, 2nd time._   **B♭5**   **B♭maj7(no3rd)/A**

_ not__ find__ a friend._   But I al - ways thought__ that I'd

Bm7   **E7**   **A**   **G5**   **G maj7(no3rd)/F♯**

1.

Gm7sus4   **Gm7**   **Csus2**

see you___ a - gain.

Em7sus4   **Em7**   **Asus2**

_mp_

Fill 2
Guitar

Guitar maintains "Asus2" until fade. (Without capo Csus2)

Sweet baby james

Words and Music by
JAMES TAYLOR

*8th note rhythms can be strummed with fingers or thumb.
**2nd Verse – ad lib. on 1st Verse line.

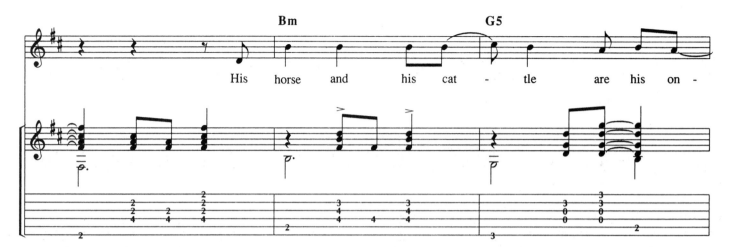

His horse and his cat - tle are his on -

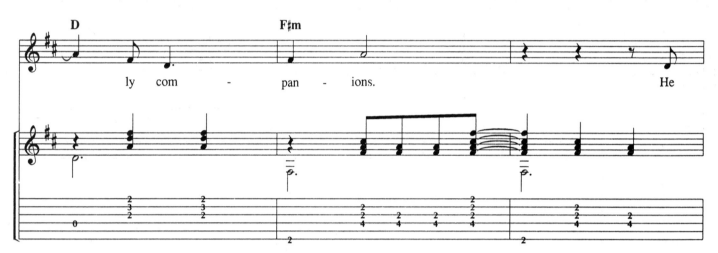

ly com - pan - ions. He

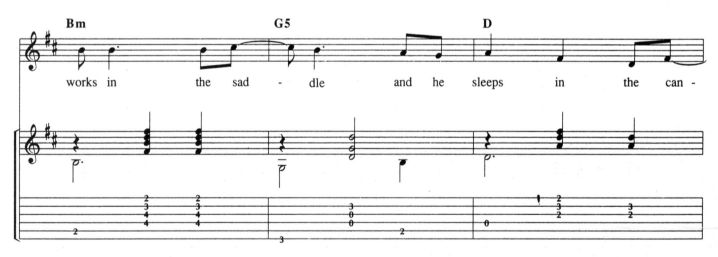

works in the sad - dle and he sleeps in the can -

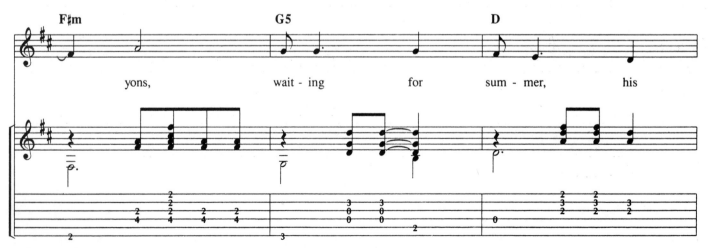

yons, wait - ing for sum - mer, his

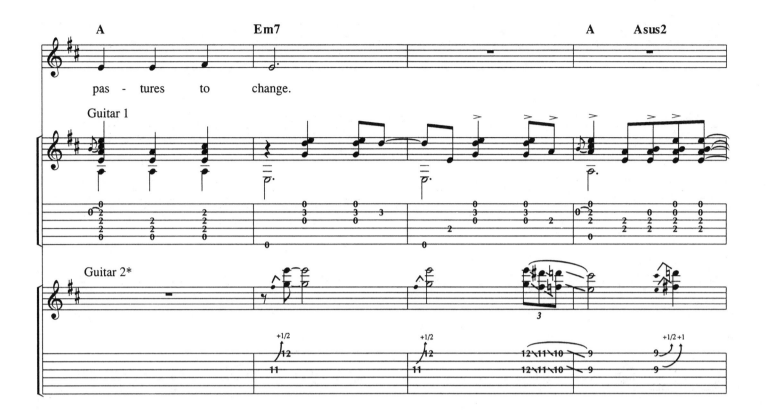

pas - tures to change.

Guitar 1

Guitar 2*

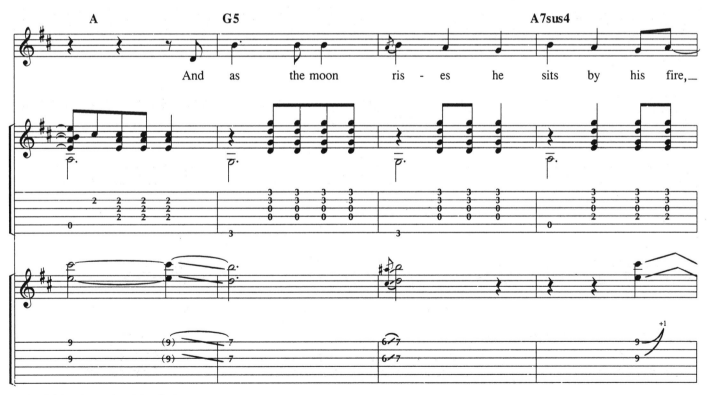

And as the moon ris - es he sits by his fire,__

Pedal Steel arranged for Guitar.

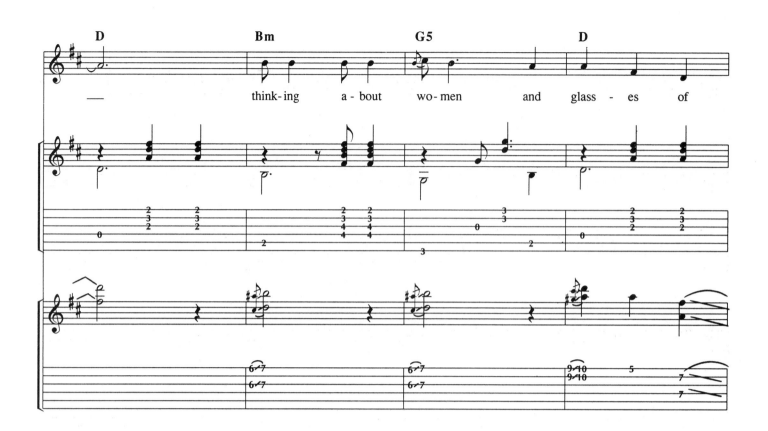

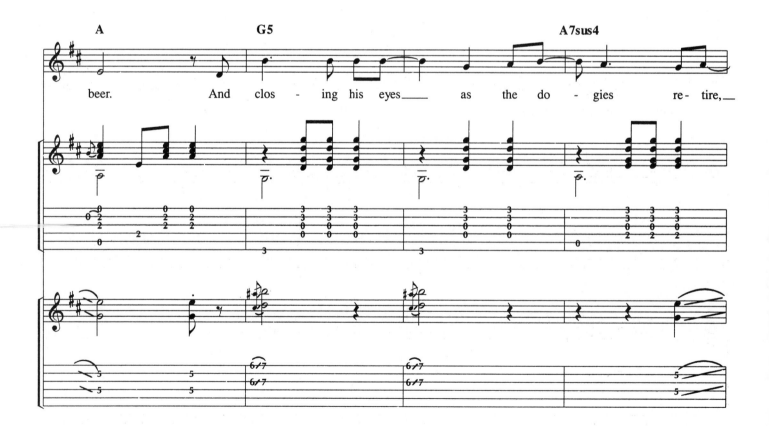

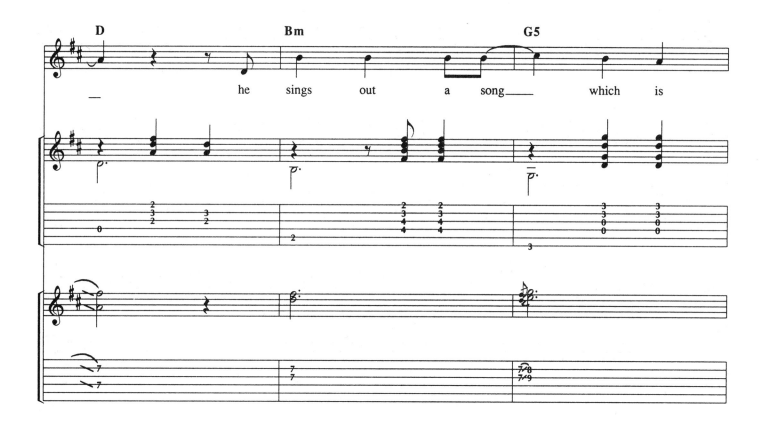

he sings out a song_____ which is

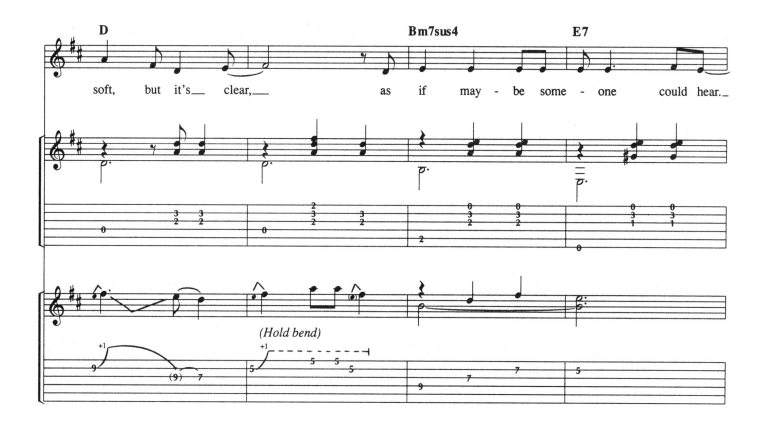

soft, but it's___ clear,___ as if may - be some - one could hear._

(Hold bend)

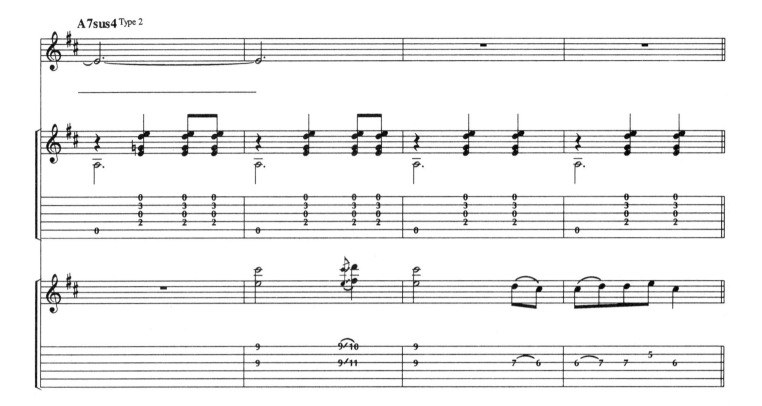

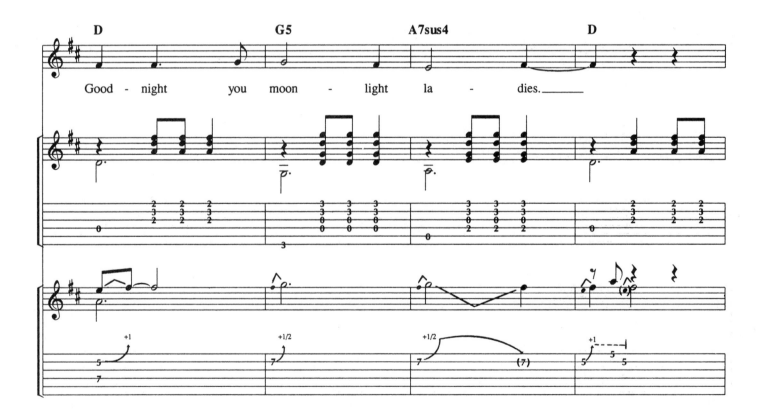

Good - night you moon - light la - dies._____

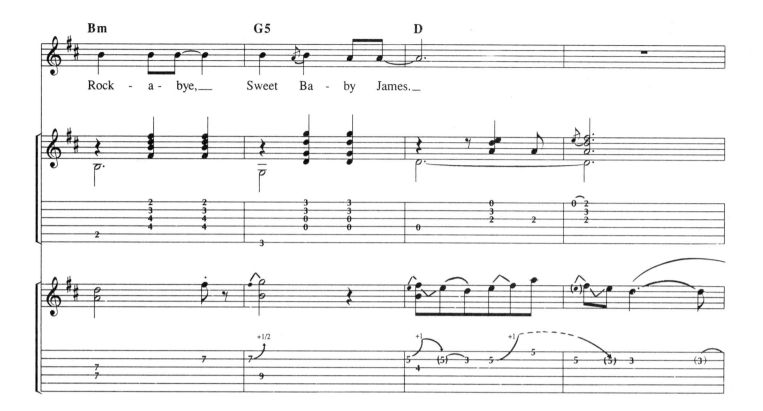

Rock - a - bye,___ Sweet Ba - by James.___

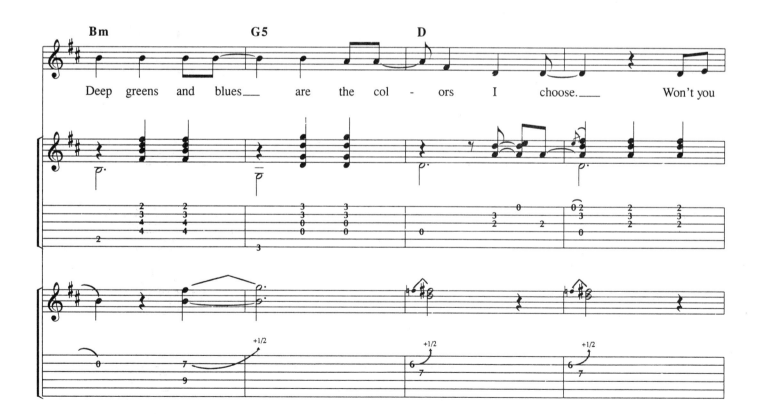

Deep greens and blues___ are the col - ors I choose.___ Won't you

let me go down___ in my___ dreams, and

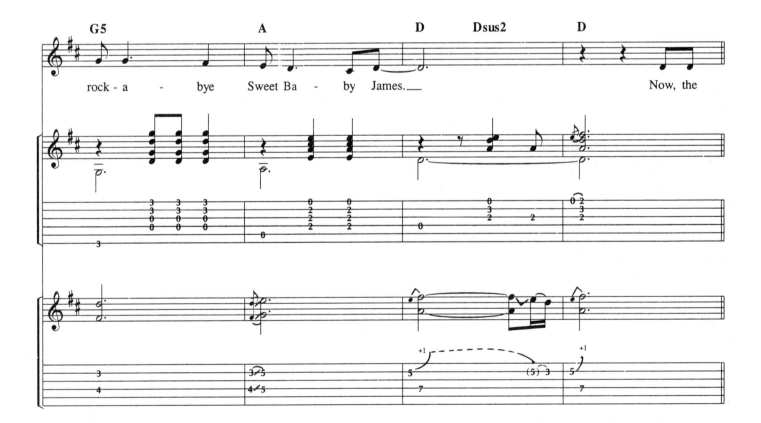

rock - a - bye Sweet Ba - by James.___ Now, the

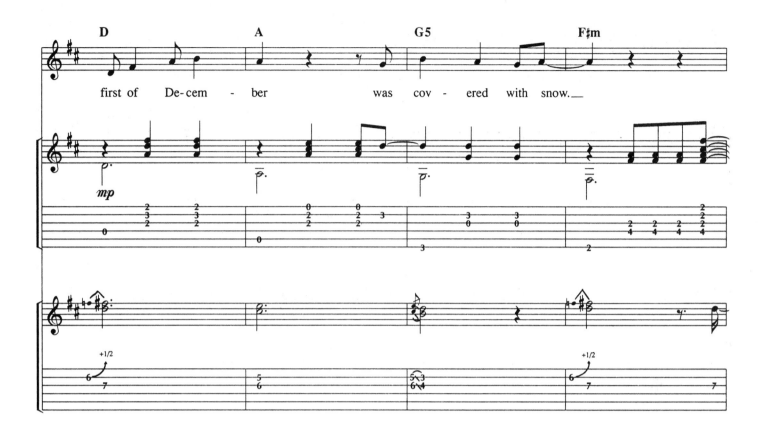

first of De-cem - ber was cov - ered with snow. ___

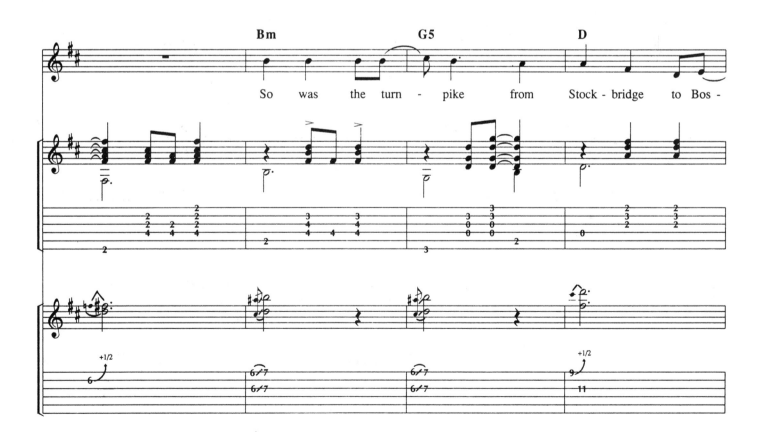

So was the turn - pike from Stock - bridge to Bos -

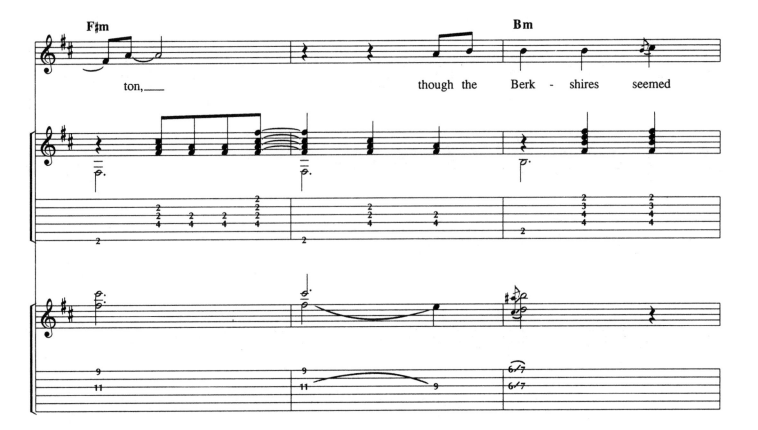

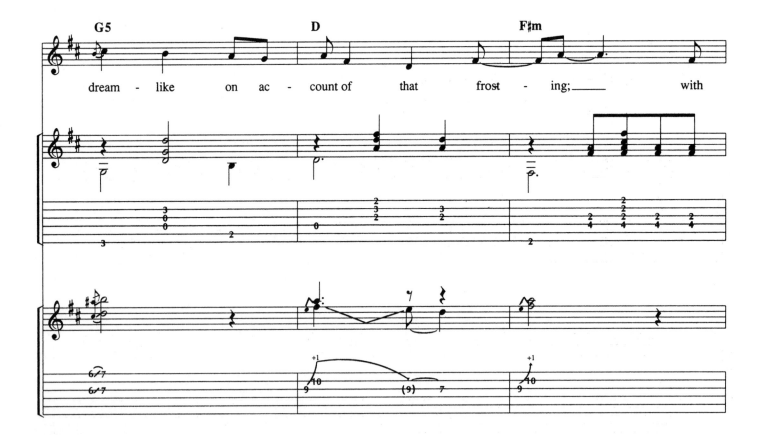

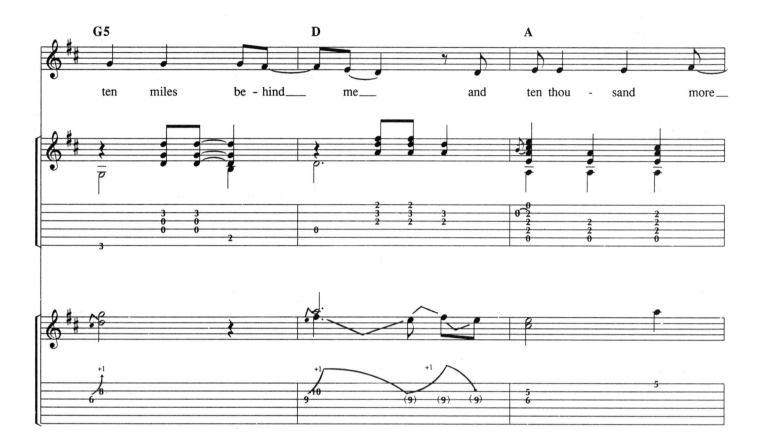

ten miles be - hind___ me___ and ten thou - sand more__

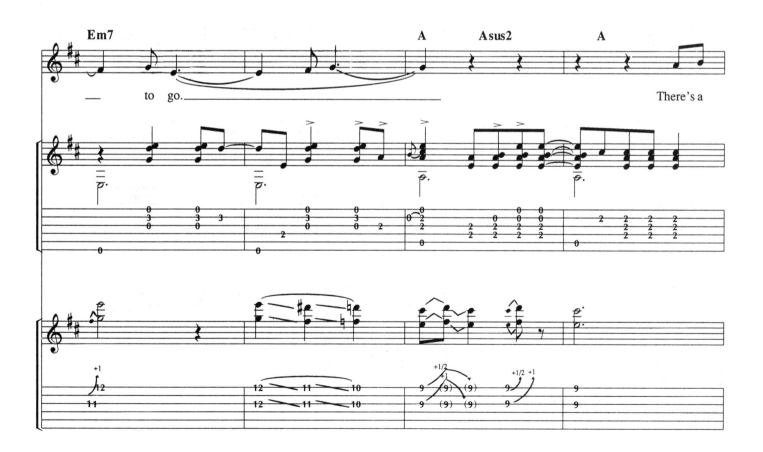

__ to go._____ There's a

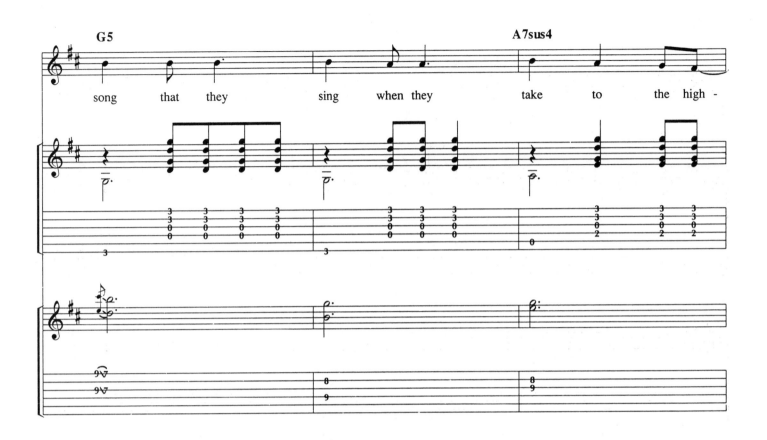

song that they sing when they take to the high -

way; a song that they sing when they take to the sea;

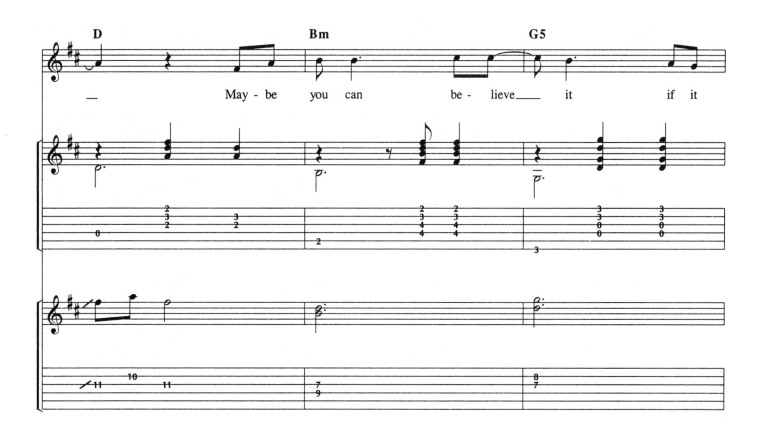

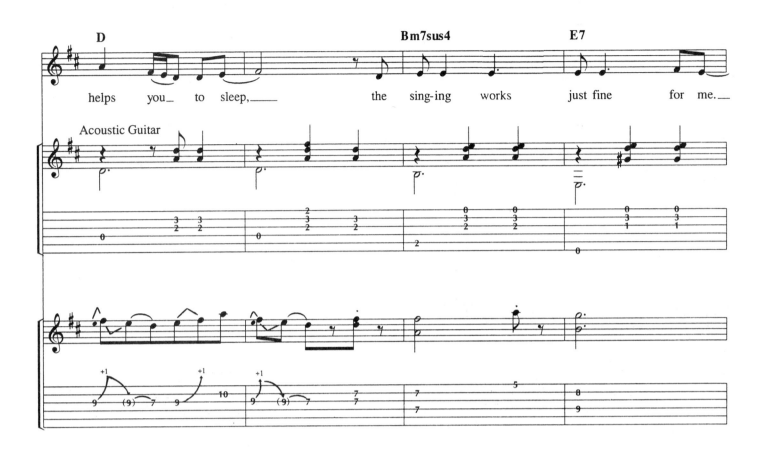

helps you to sleep,_____ the sing-ing works just fine for me._____

So___

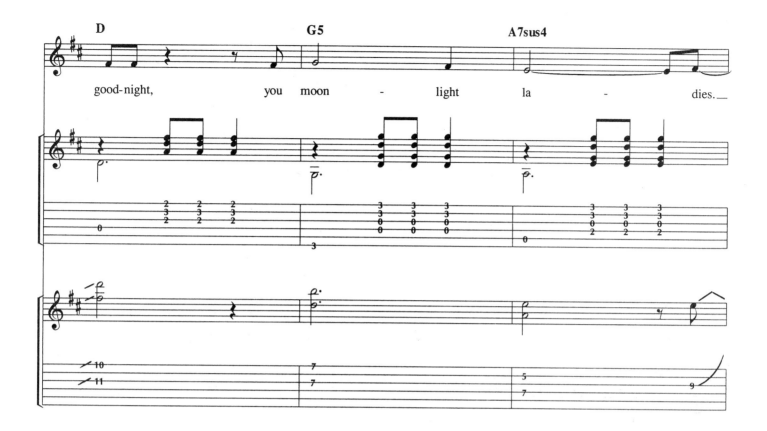

good-night, you moon - light la - dies.___

___ Rock - a - bye,___ Sweet Ba - by James.___

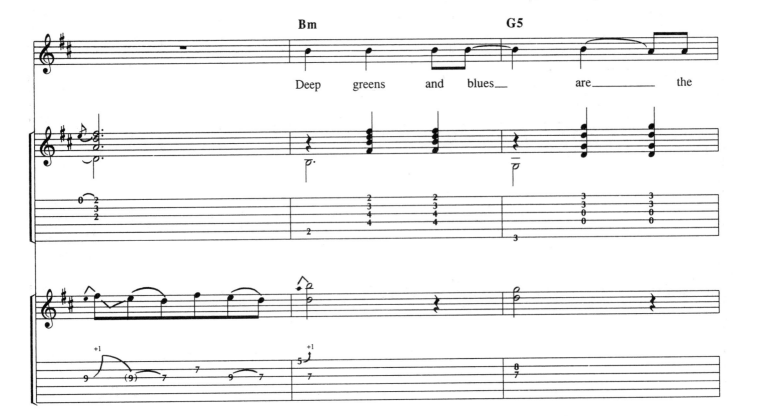

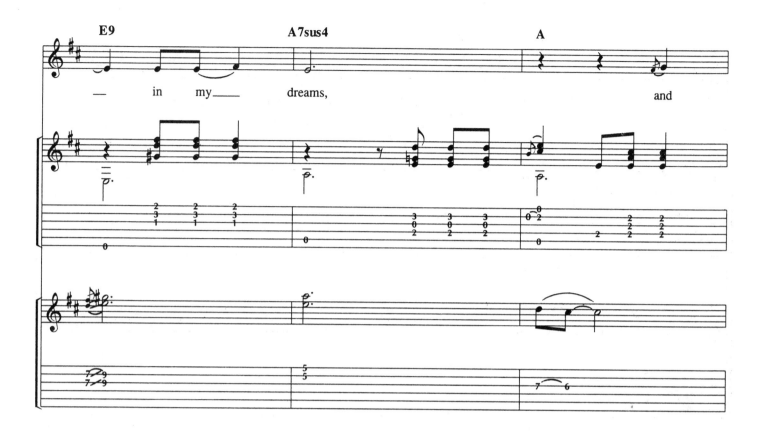

— in my____ dreams, _____ and

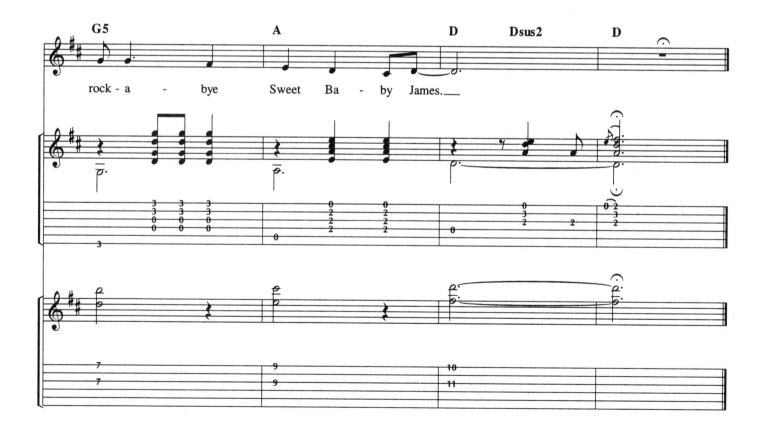

rock - a - bye Sweet Ba - by James.____

Country road

Words and Music by
JAMES TAYLOR

D   C/D   G/D   Em7   A7   Bm

F/D   G   G/A   C/A   C   C/B

Moderately ♩ = 74

*Guitar 1
legato
mf

Take to the high - way won't you lend me— your— name?—

*Tune 6 string to D

*On D.S. only.

On a coun - try road.____

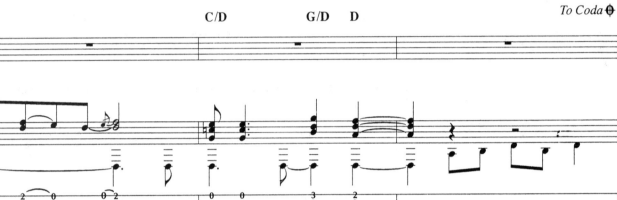

To Coda ⊕

Verse 2:

Sail on____ home to Je - sus won't you good girls____ and____ boys.____

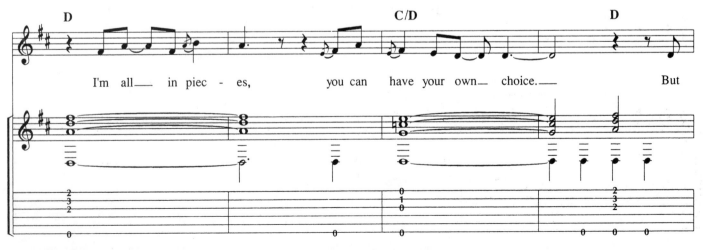

I'm all____ in piec - es, you can have your own____ choice.____ But

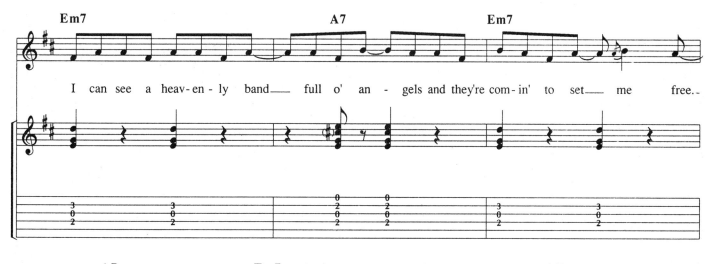

I can see a heav-en-ly band___ full o' an - gels and they're com-in' to set___ me free.___

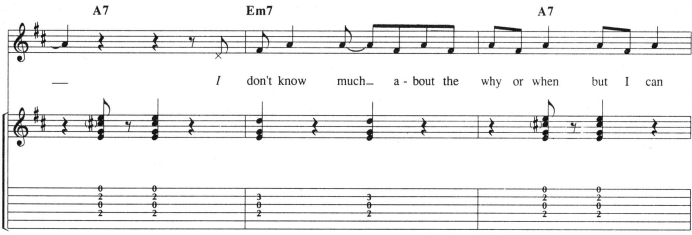

___ I don't know much___ a - bout the why or when but I can

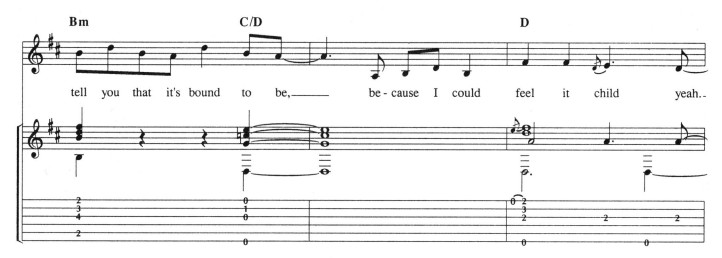

tell you that it's bound to be,_____ be - cause I could feel it child yeah..

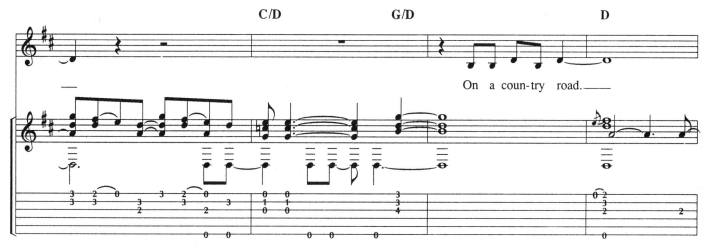

On a coun-try road.___

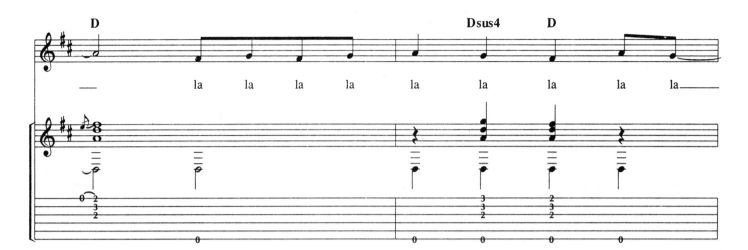

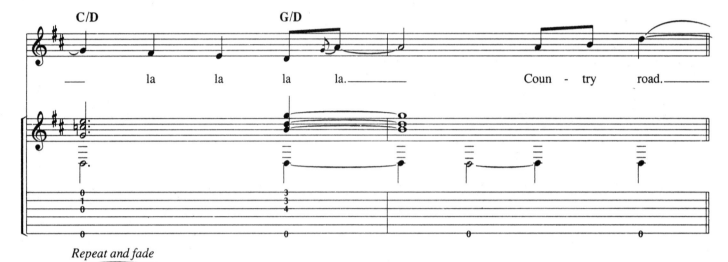

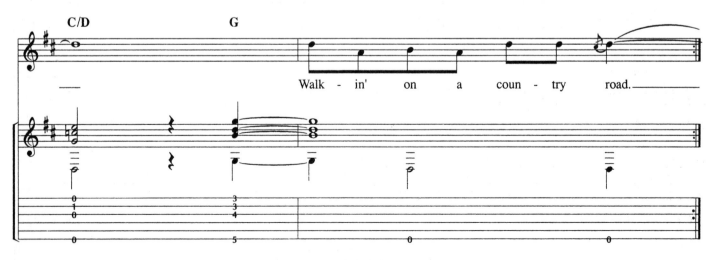

You've got a friend

Words and Music by
CAROLE KING

*Capo on 2nd fret.

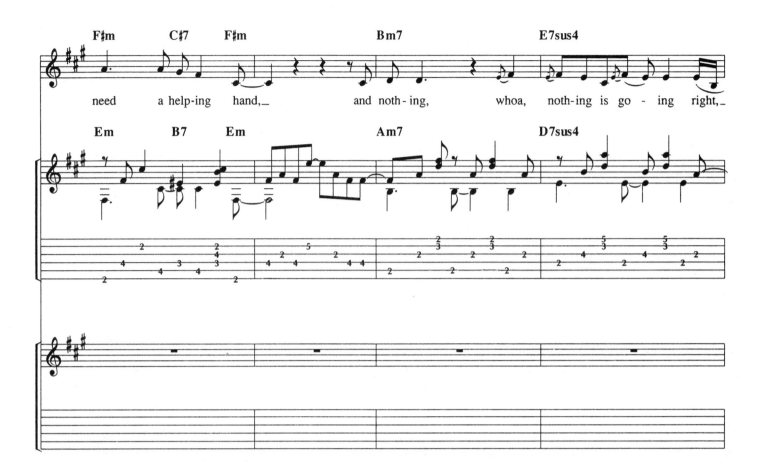

need a help-ing hand,__ and noth-ing, whoa, noth-ing is go - ing right,__

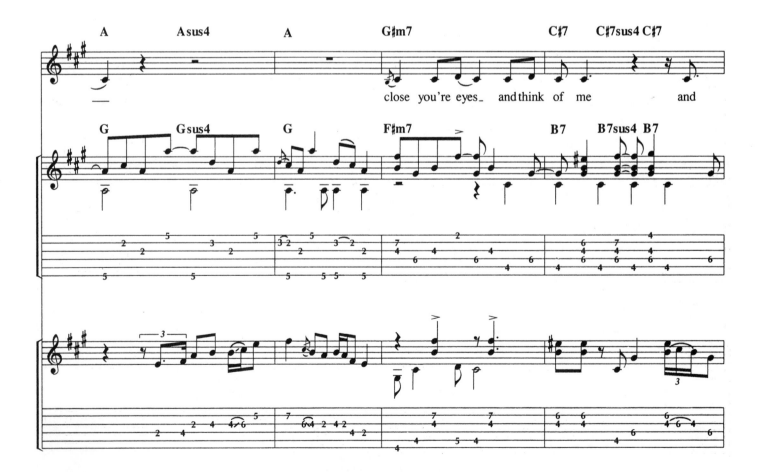

close you're eyes__ and think of me and

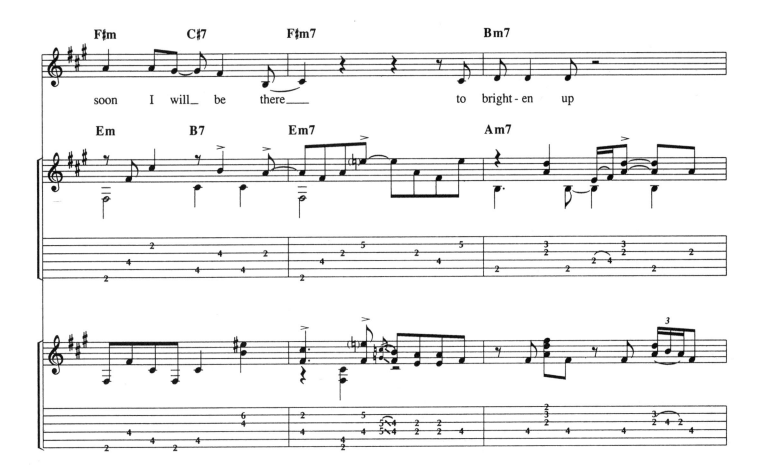

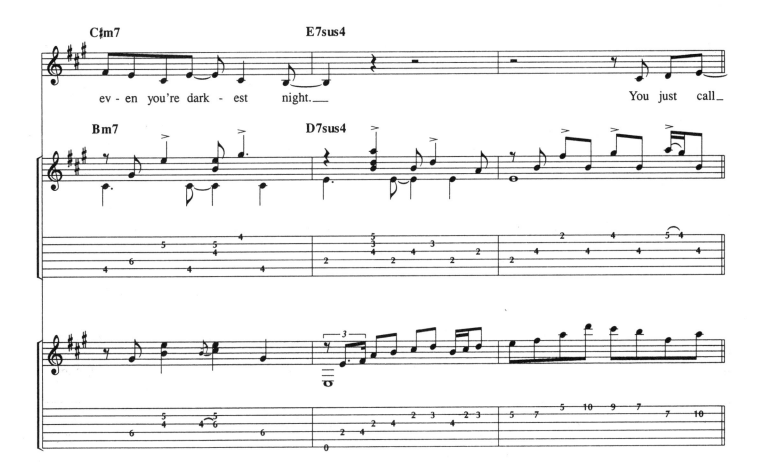

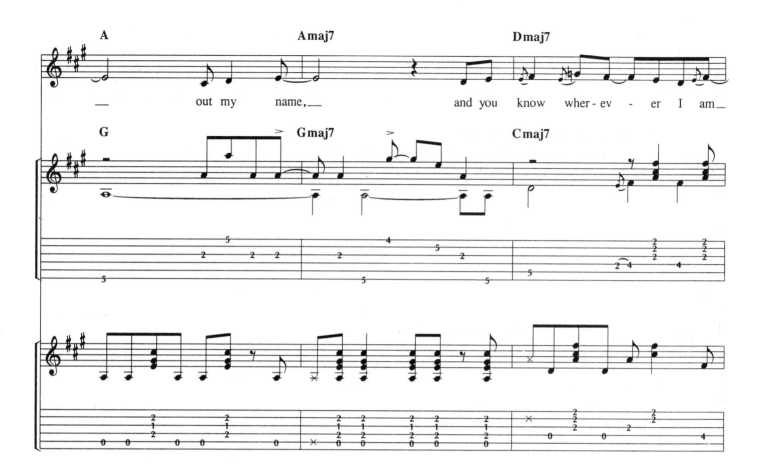

out my name,_____ and you know wher - ev - er I am____

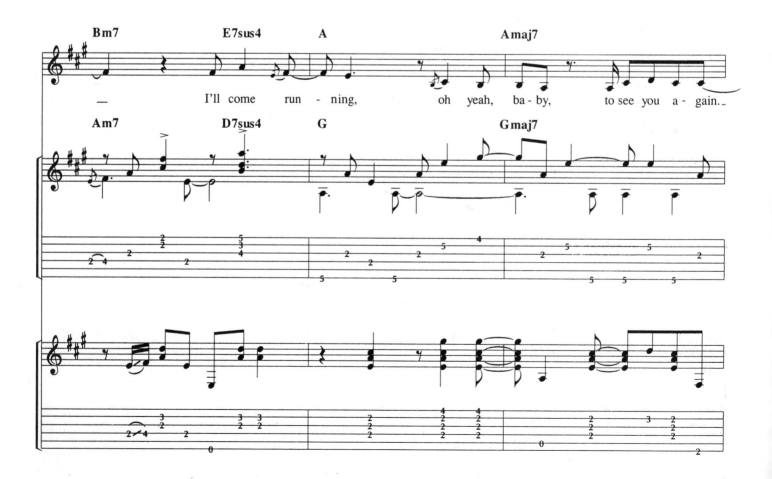

I'll come run - ning, oh yeah, ba - by, to see you a - gain.___

Win-ter, spring, sum-mer, or fall,

all you got to do is___ call,___ and I'll

be there,___ yeah, yeah, yeah.__ You've got a friend. __

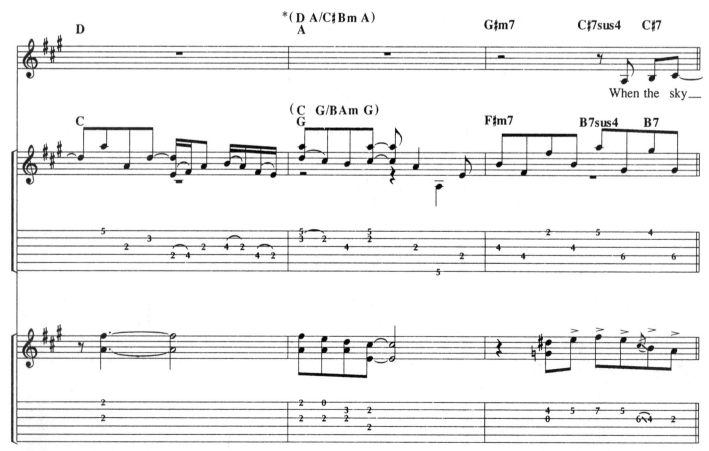

When the sky__

Harmony implied by Bass.

keep your head__ to - geth - er   and

call my name_____ out__ loud,_____ now.   Soon I'll be knock-

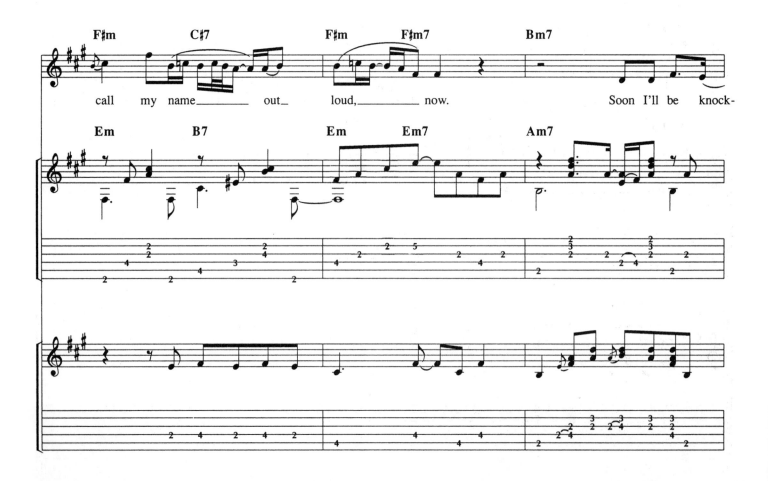

67

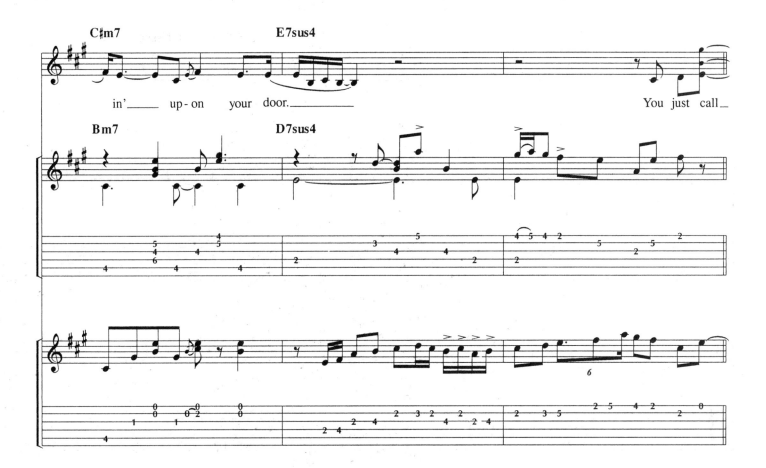

ing,___ oh yes, I will, *to* see you a - gain.___

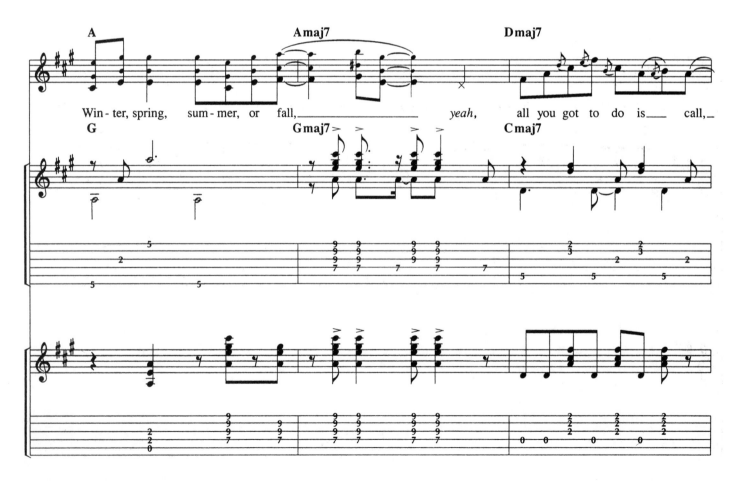

Win - ter, spring, sum - mer, or fall,___ *yeah,* all you got to do is___ call,___

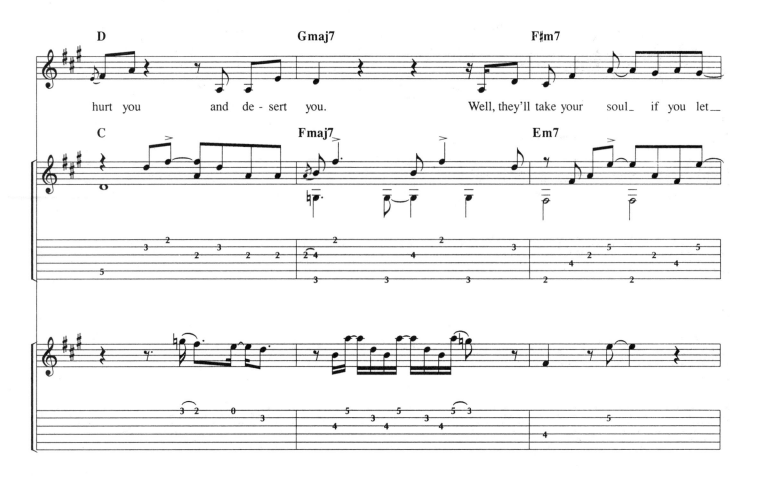

hurt you and de-sert you. Well, they'll take your soul_ if you let_

_ them. Oh, yeah, but don't_ you let them. You just call_ out my name,.

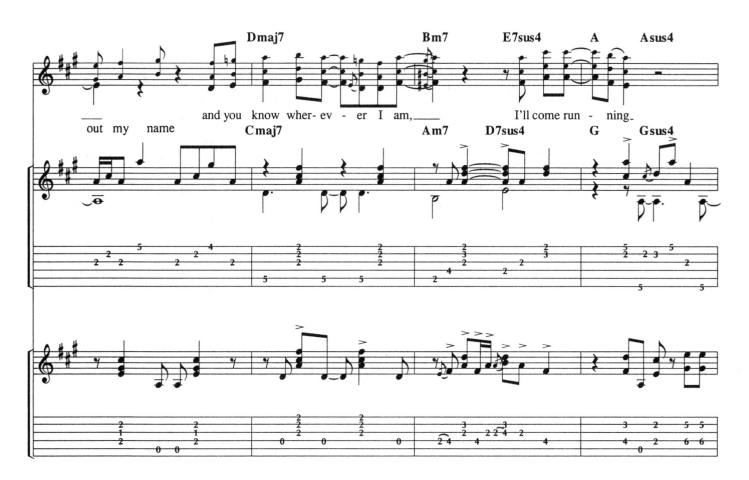

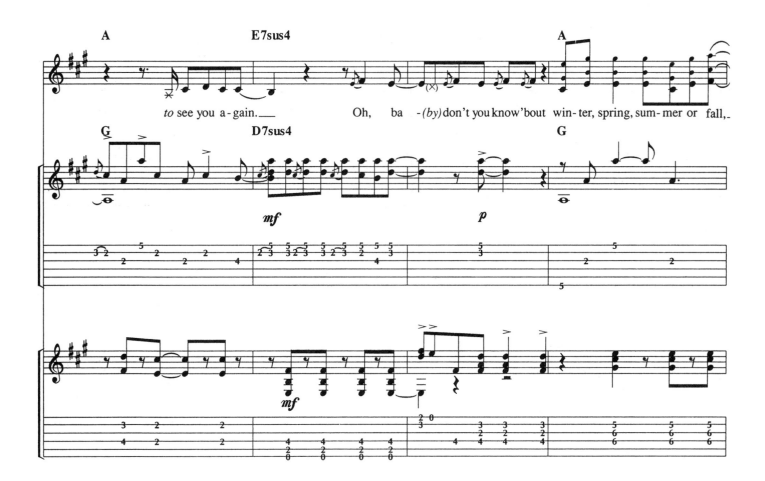

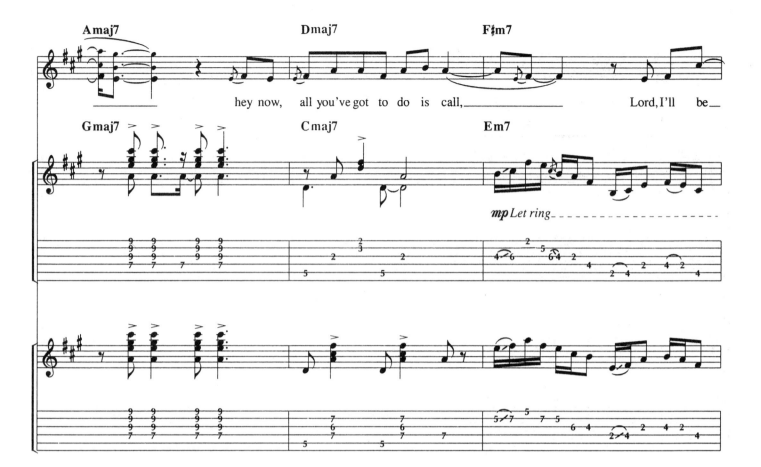

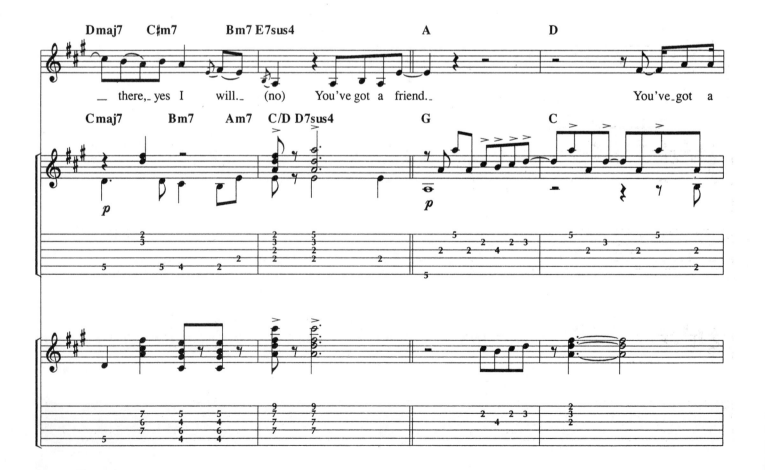

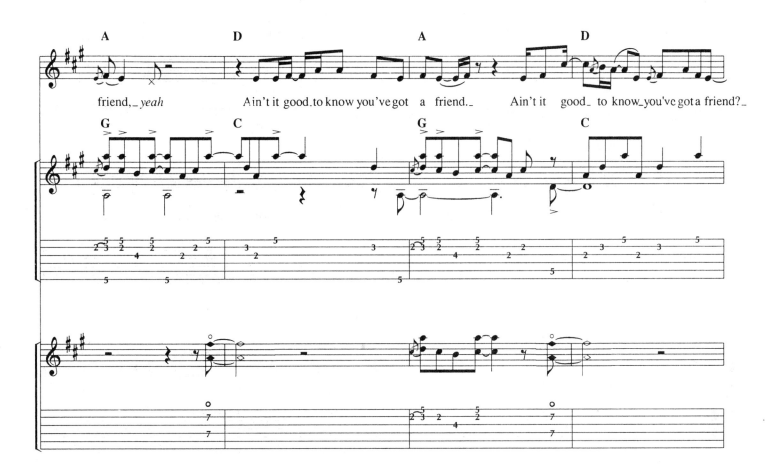

friend, _ yeah   Ain't it good to know you've got a friend. _   Ain't it good_ to know_you've got a friend?_

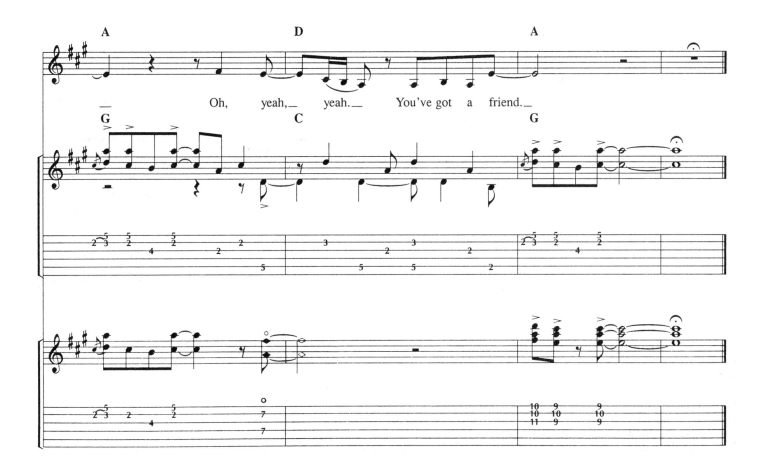

Oh,   yeah,_   yeah._   You've got a friend._

Don't let me be lonely tonight

Words and Music by
JAMES TAYLOR

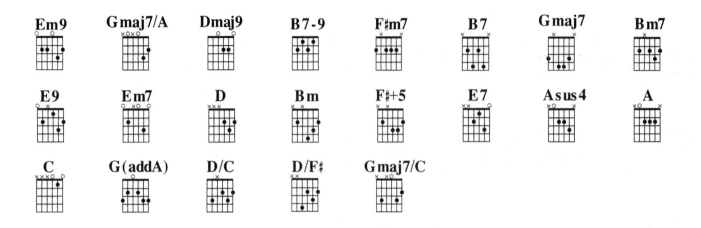

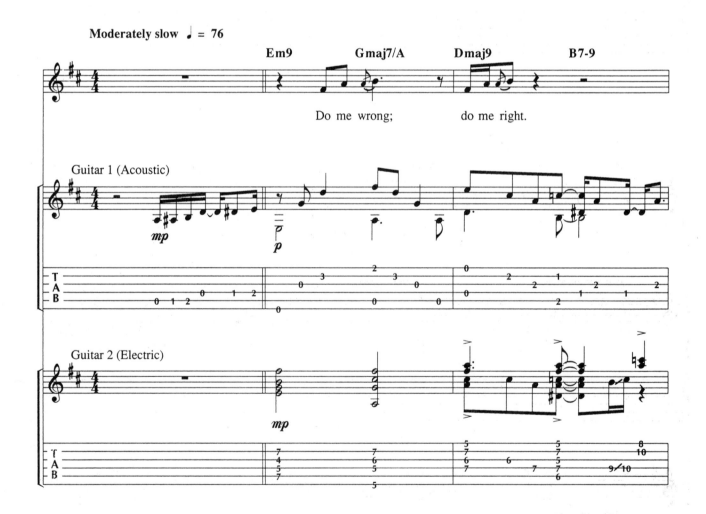

Tell me lies,__ but hold__ me tight.__ Save your good-byes for__ the morn-

ing light,__ but don't let me be lone - ly to - night.__

Say good-bye and say— hel-lo.—— *It's* sure 'nough good— *to* see— you, but it's

time to go.— Don't say yes but— please don't say— no.— I don't

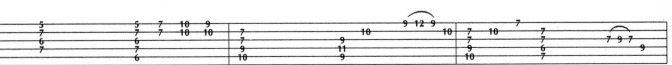

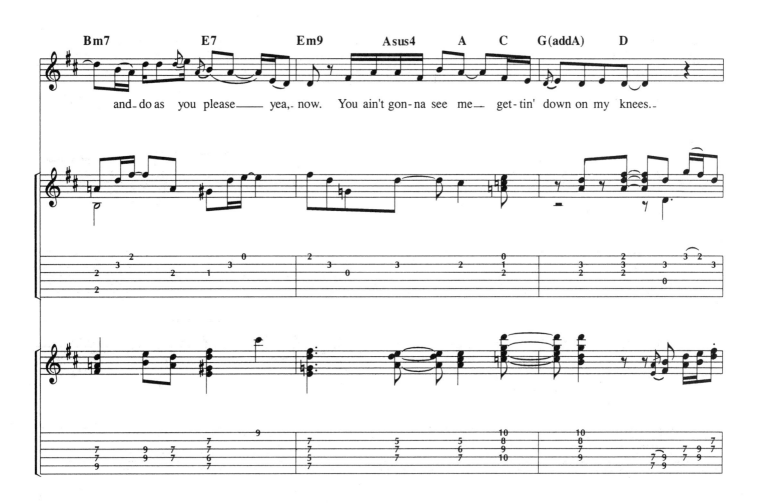

I'm un-de-cid-ed and your heart's been di-vid-ed. You've been turn-ing my world up-side down, no, no.___ So do me wrong;

do me right,. right now_ ba - by.   Go on and tell me lies   but hold   me tight.____

Save your good-byes for the morn - in' light   morn-in' light,_ but don't   let me be lone-ly to-night.

I don't want to be lone-ly to-night. No,___ no__ I don't

want to__ be lone-ly _to_-night.__

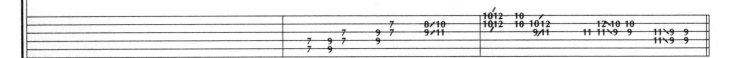

Walking man

Words and Music by
JAMES TAYLOR

* *Open sixth string optional*

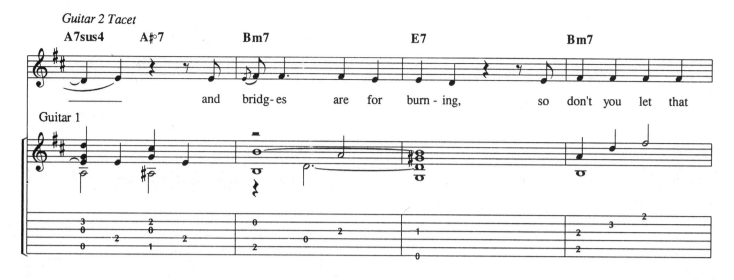

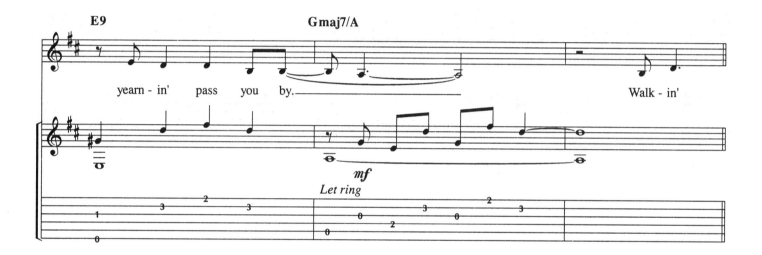

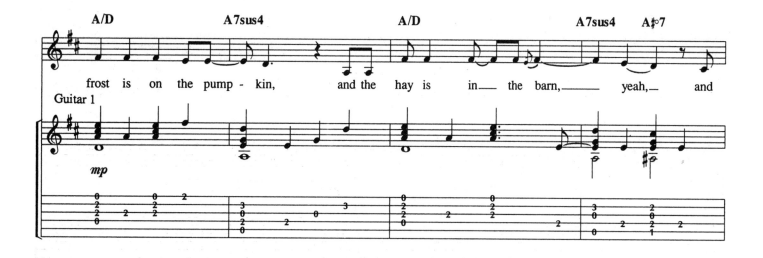

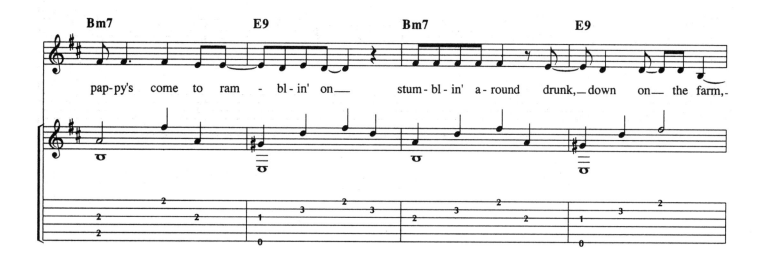

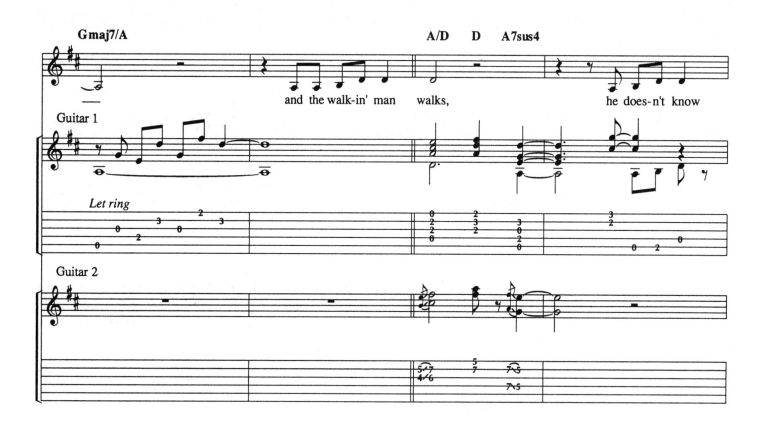

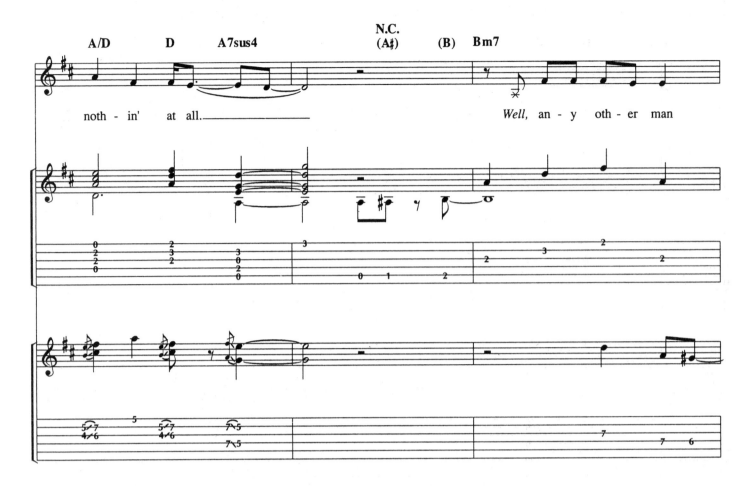

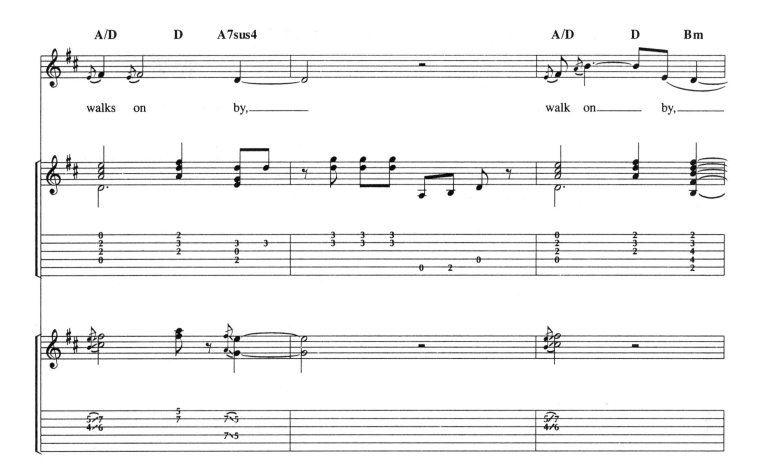

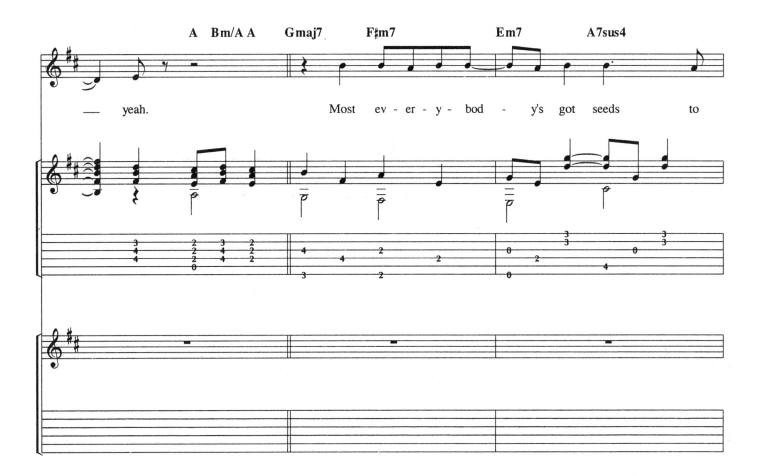

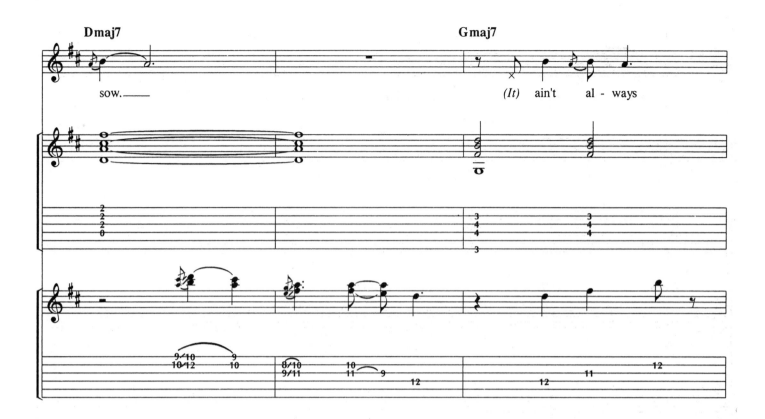

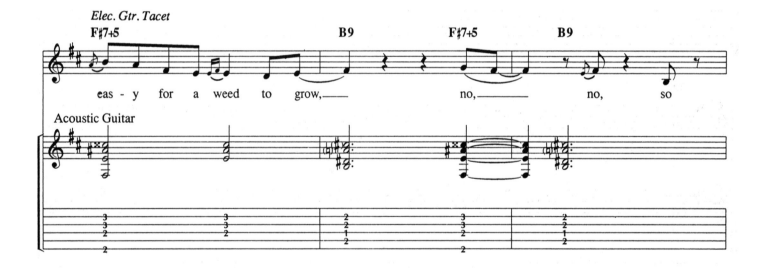

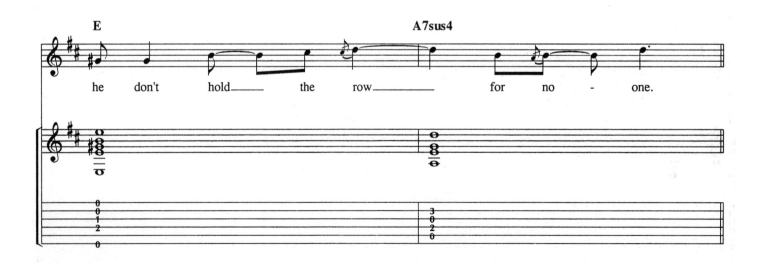

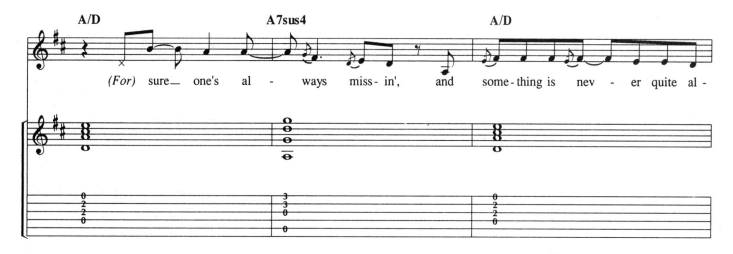

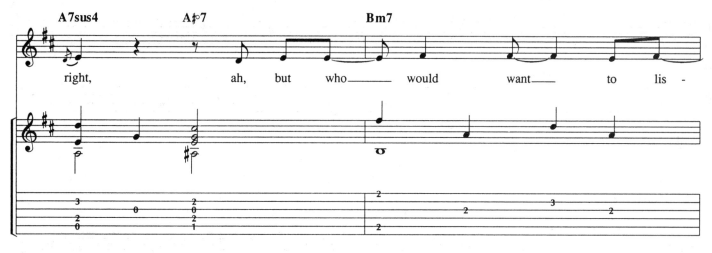

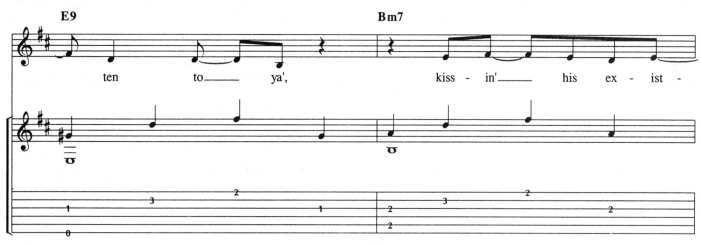

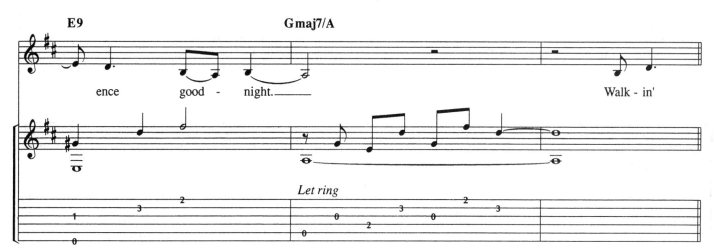

*Acoustic Guitar overdub.

How sweet it is (to be loved by you)

Words and Music by
EDDIE HOLLAND,
LAMONT DOZIER and BRIAN HOLLAND

*Piano arranged for Guitar.

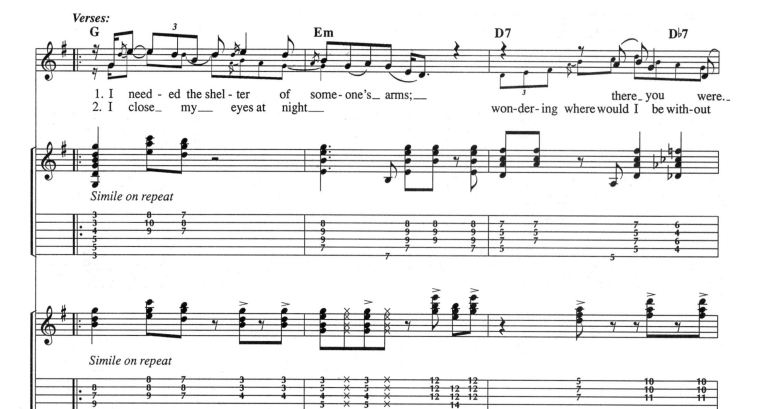

Verses:

1. I need - ed the shel - ter of some - one's arms; there you were.
2. I close my eyes at night won-der-ing where would I be with-out

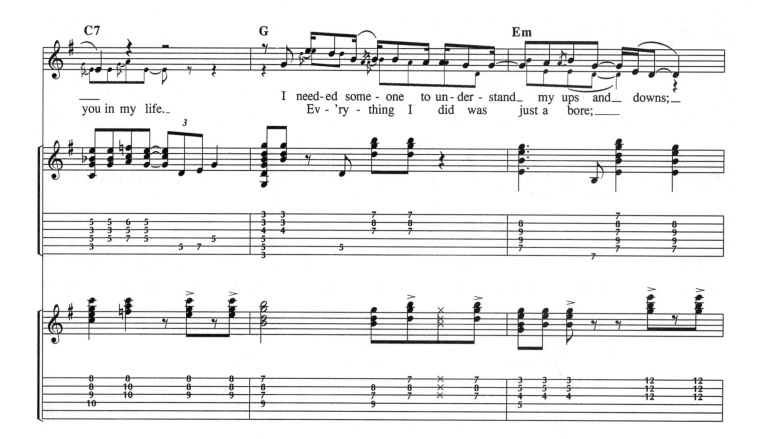

you in my life.
I need-ed some - one to un-der-stand my ups and downs;
Ev - 'ry - thing I did was just a bore;

ev - 'ry - where I went seems I'd been there be - fore. But

With Fill 1 on D.S.

With_ sweet_ love an' de - vo - tion_ deep - ly touch - ing my e - mo-
you bright - en up for me all_ of my days_ with a_ love so sweet in
See additional lyrics

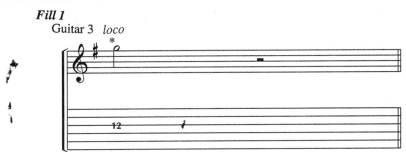

Fill 1
Guitar 3 *loco*

End of Sax solo

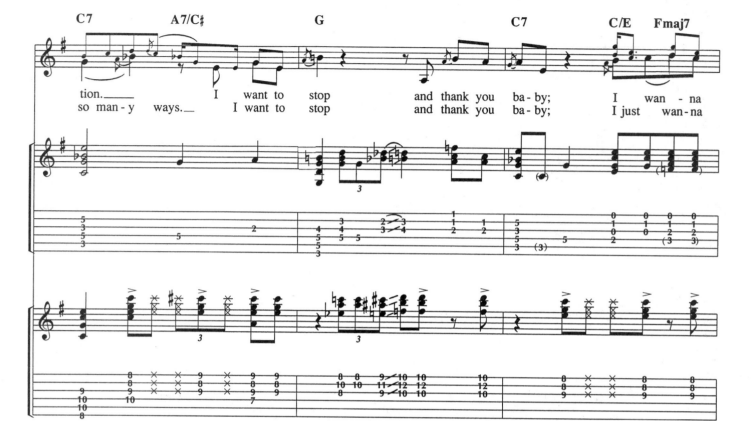

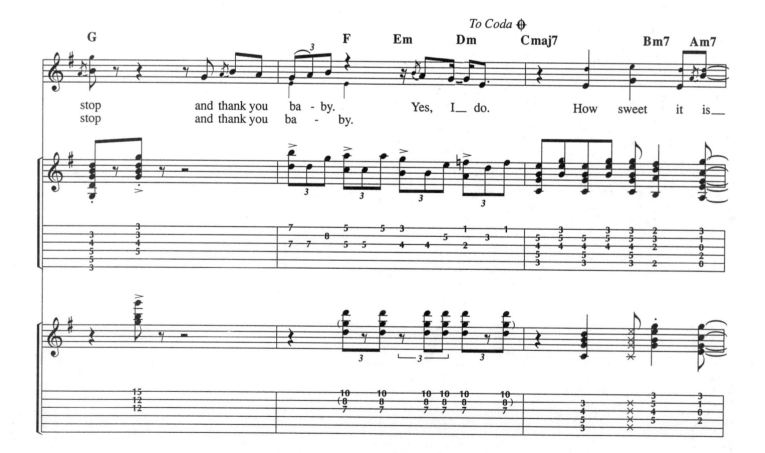

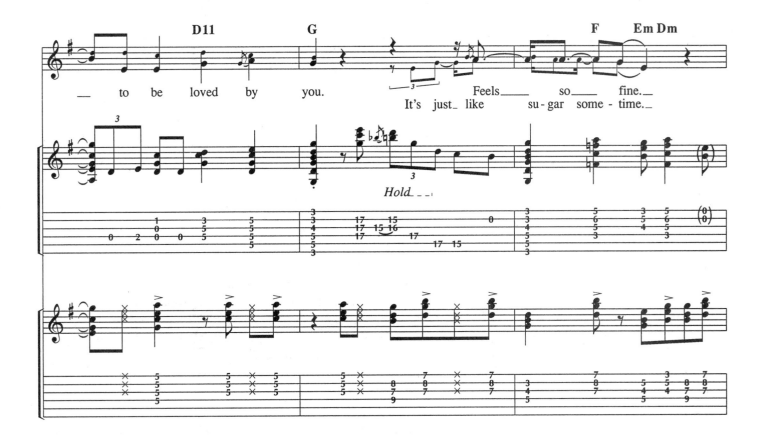

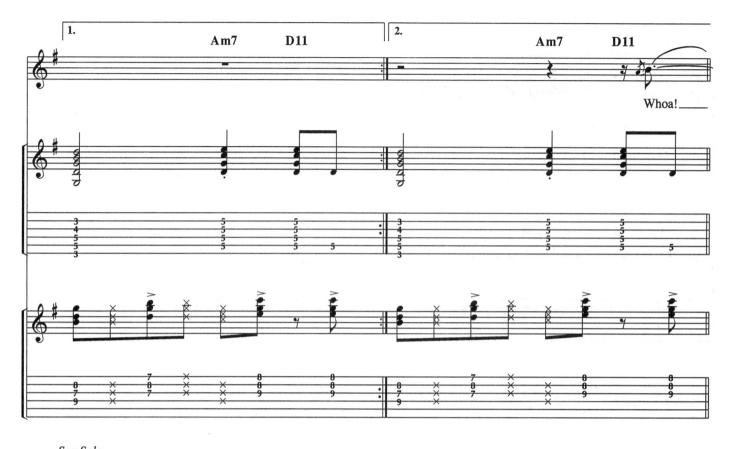

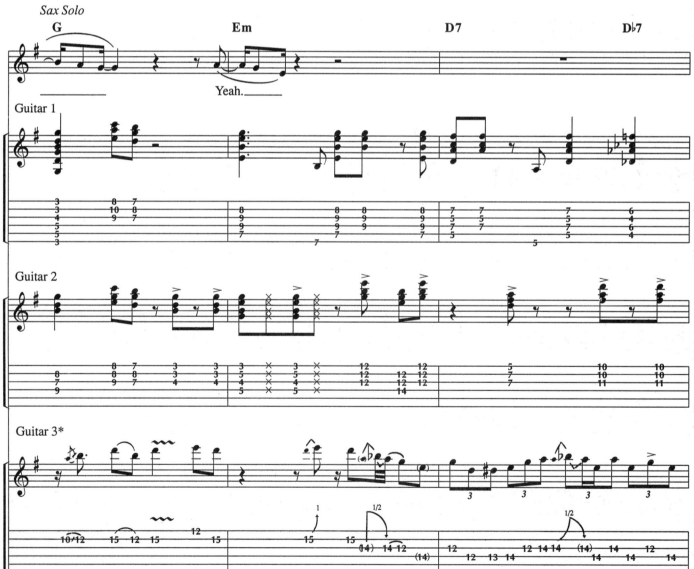

*Sax arranged for Guitar.

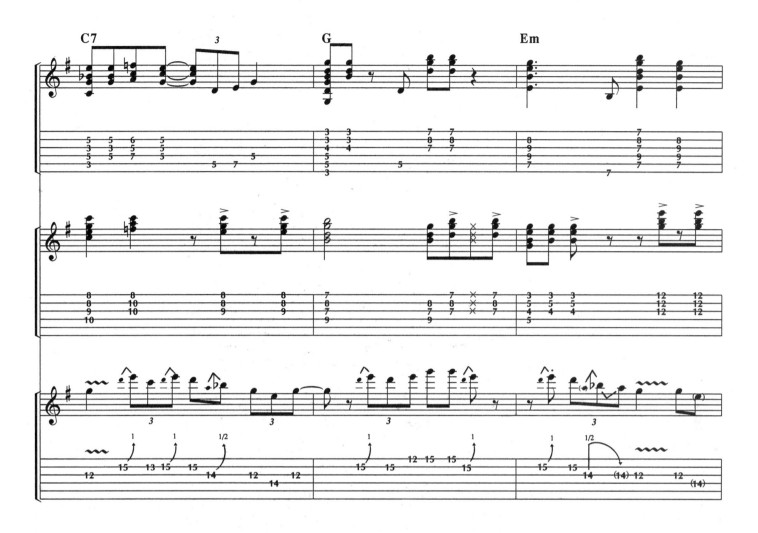

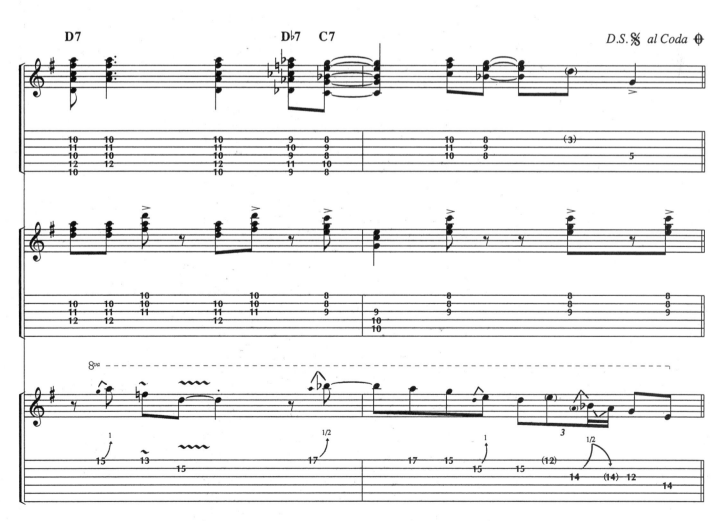

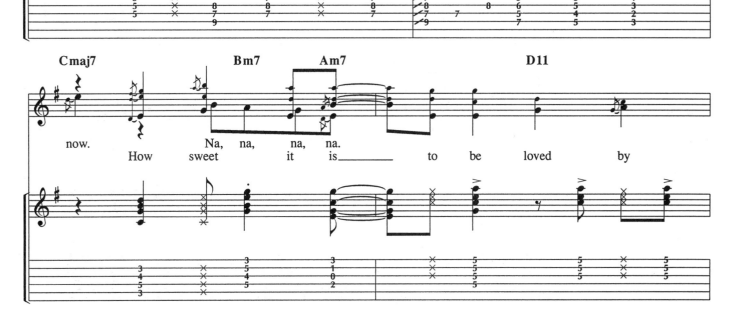

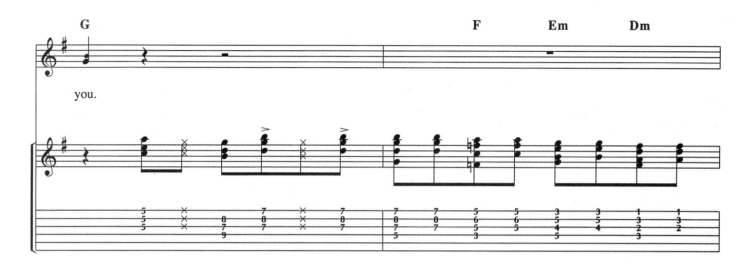

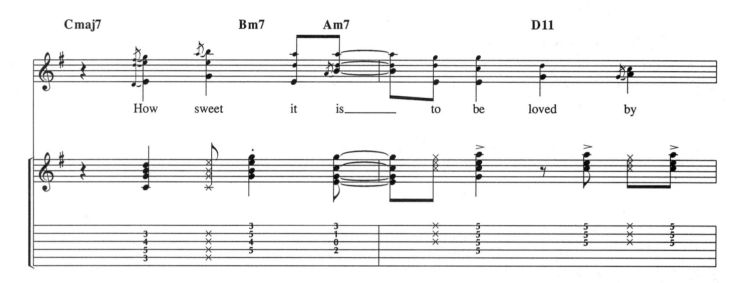

Additional Lyrics

You were better to me than I was to myself;
For me there's you and there ain't nobody else.
I want to . . .

Mexico

Words and Music by
JAMES TAYLOR

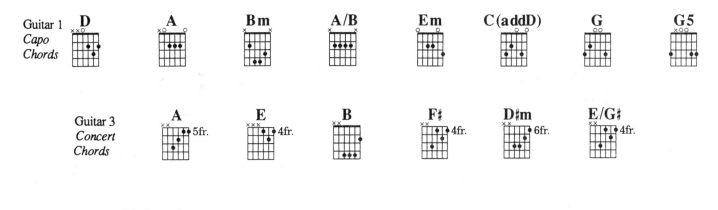

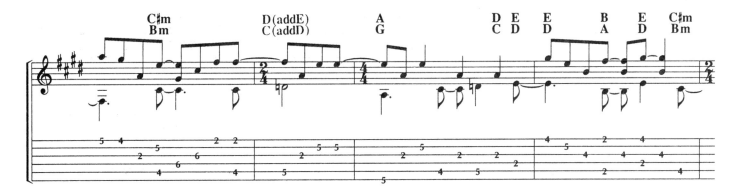

*Capo at 2nd fret. Two acoustic guitars arranged as one.

Ba-by's hun - gry and the mon-ey's all gone. *The* folks back home don't want to

talk on the phone.__ *She* gets a long letter, sends back__ a post-card;__ times are hard.

Shower the people

Words and Music by
JAMES TAYLOR

*Capo at 3rd fret.

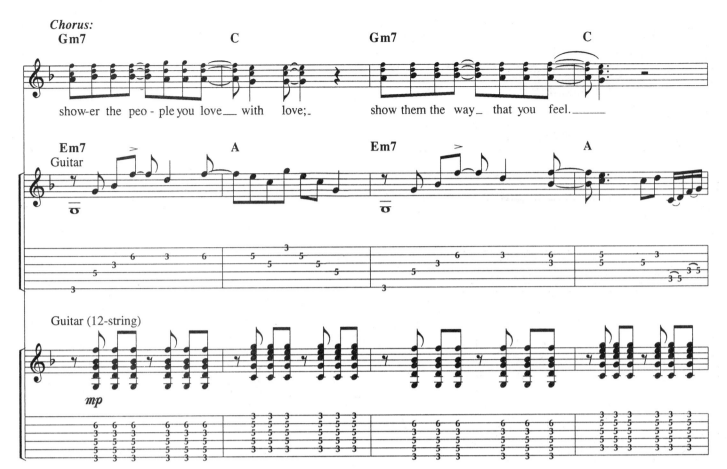

Chorus:

show-er the peo-ple you love___ with love;___ show them the way___ that you feel._____

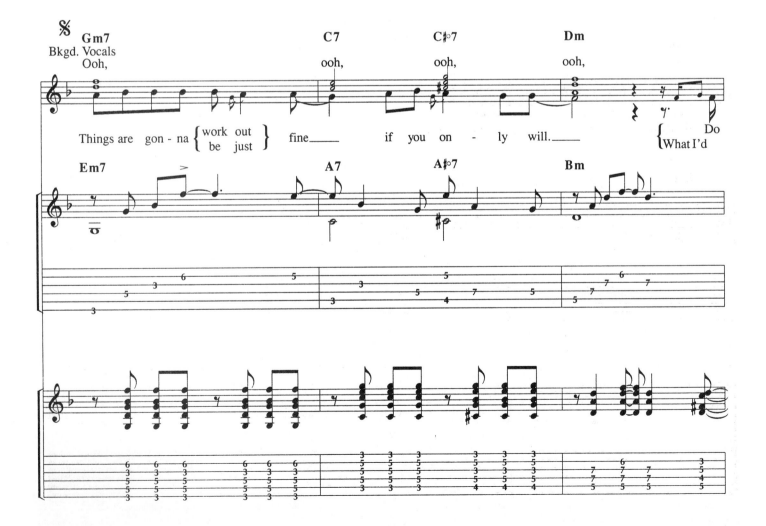

Things are gon-na {work out / be just} fine___ if you on-ly will.___ {Do / What I'd}

Played by Bass.

tell some-bod-y the way__ that you feel__ you can feel it be-gin-ning to ease.__ I think it's true__

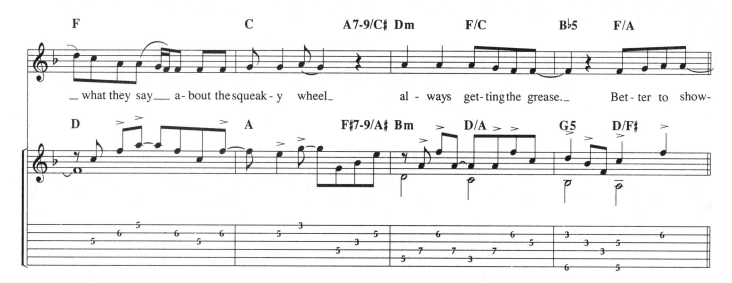

__ what they say__ a-bout the squeak-y wheel__ al-ways get-ting the grease.__ Bet-ter to show-

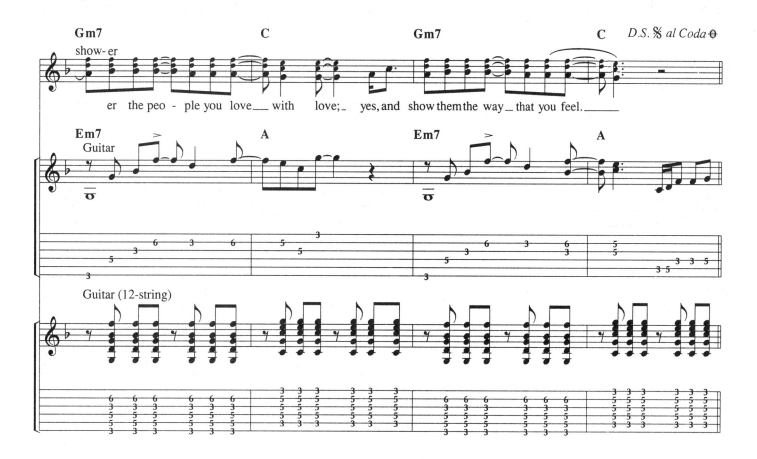

show-er
er the peo-ple you love__ with love;__ yes, and show them the way__ that you feel._____

Additional Lyrics

Ad lib. Vocal:
They say in every life,
They say the rain must fall.
Just like the pouring rain,
Make it rain.

Love is sunshine.
Love, love love is sunshine.
Make it rain
Love, love love is sunshine. Alright, yeah.
Everybody, everybody, everybody, everybody.

Steamroller

Words and Music by
JAMES TAYLOR

*Capo at 3rd fret. The number 3 in tab represents a capoed open string.

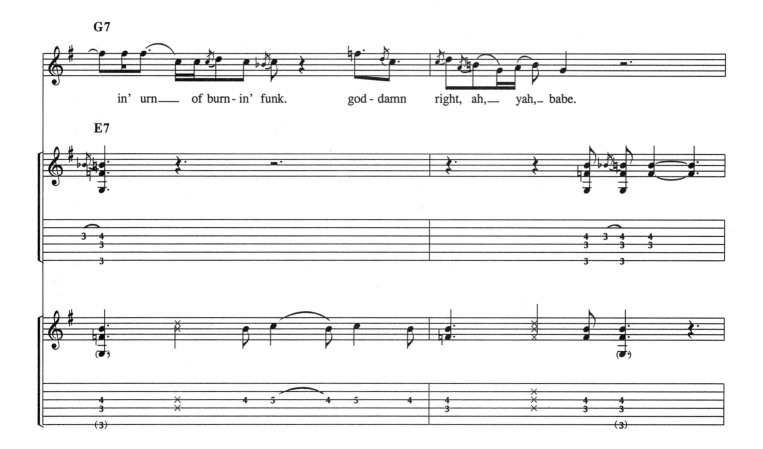

Well, I'm a dem-o-li-tion der-by, ba-by, yeah   a hef-ty_ hunk of steam-ing junk._

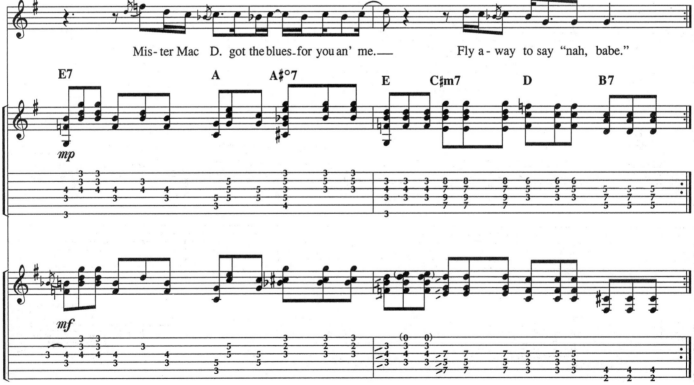

Mis-ter Mac D. got the blues_for you an' me.__   Fly a-way to say "nah, babe."

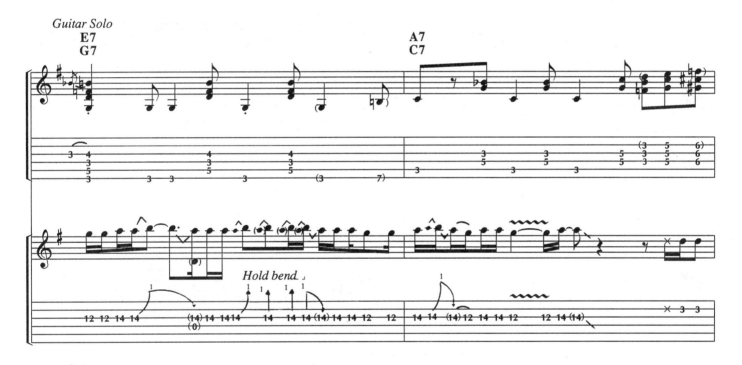

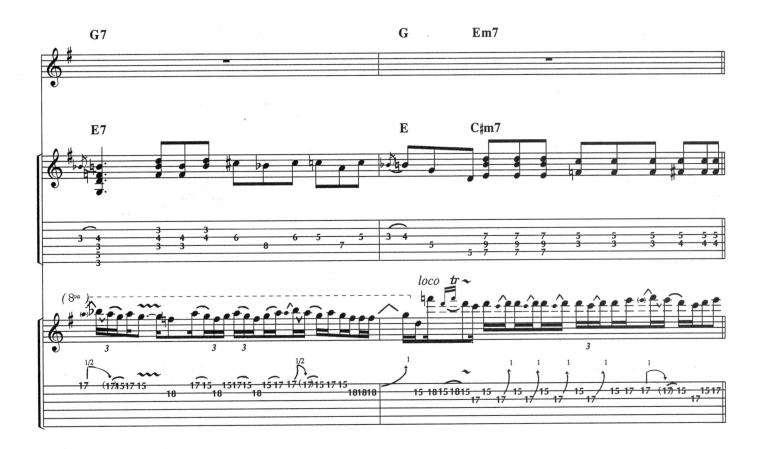

Well, I'm a na - palm bomb for you, ba - by.

Stone

G7

guar - an - teed___ to blow your mind___ high - er.

Drop a

E7

cresc. poco a poco

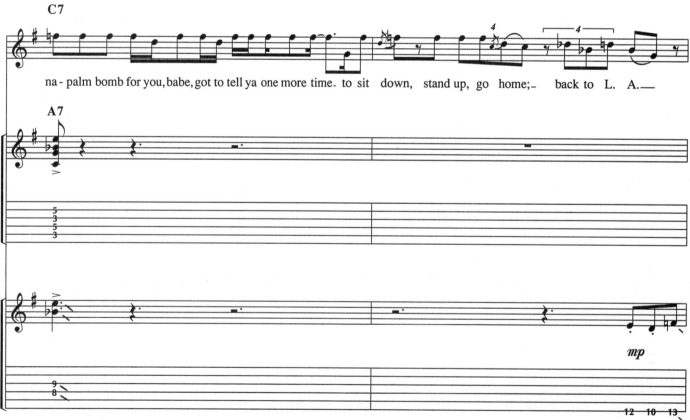

C7

na - palm bomb for you, babe, got to tell ya one more time. to sit down, stand up, go home;— back to L. A.___

A7

mp

12 10 13

Stone guar-an - teed———————— to blow your mind ma-ma, yeah.——— And—

— if I can't—have you first for my own to take home an' keep me warm; there won't be noth-in' left be-hind._

Freely
Outro:

Oh, bo-ca-non,— bo-ca-non— boy.   I just don't seem to, can't lose———

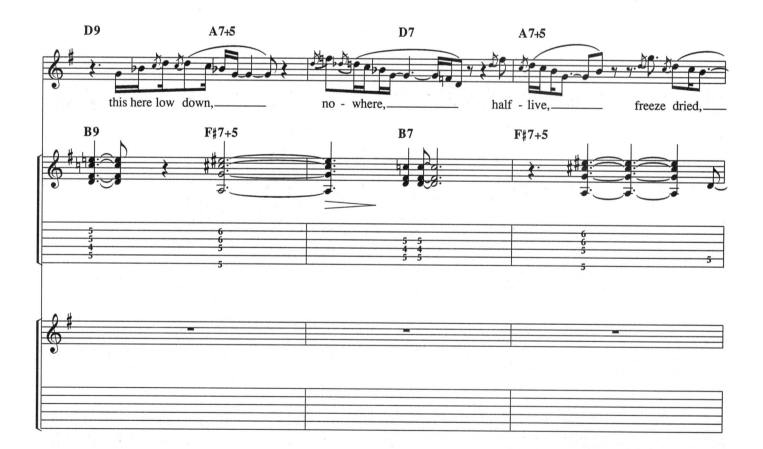

this here low down,——— no-where,——— half-live,——— freeze dried,———

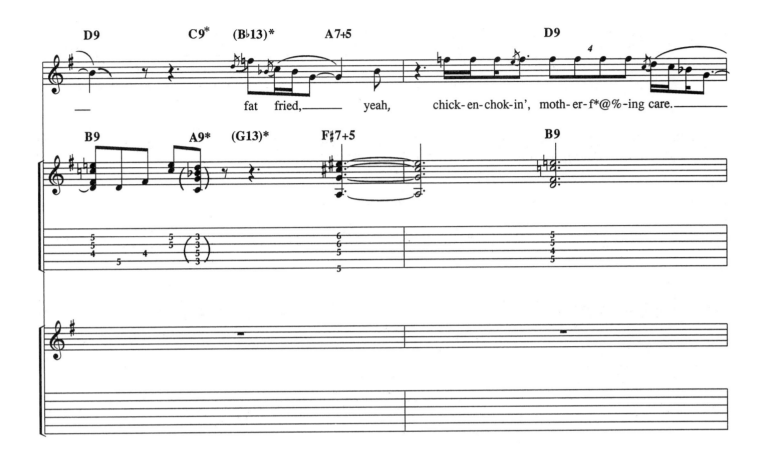

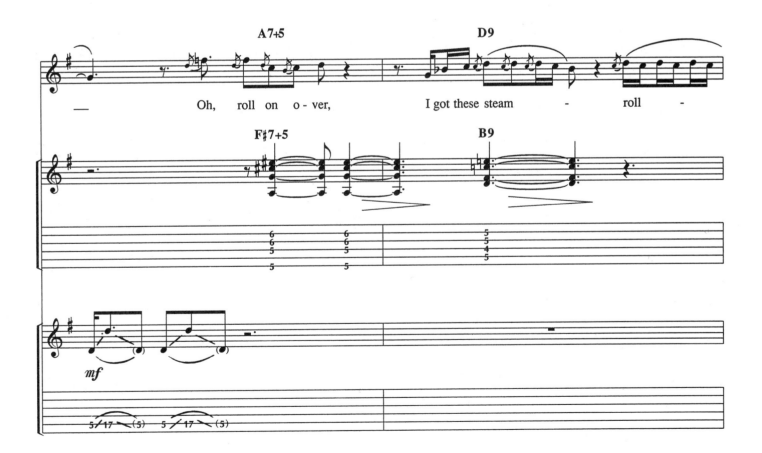

*Piano

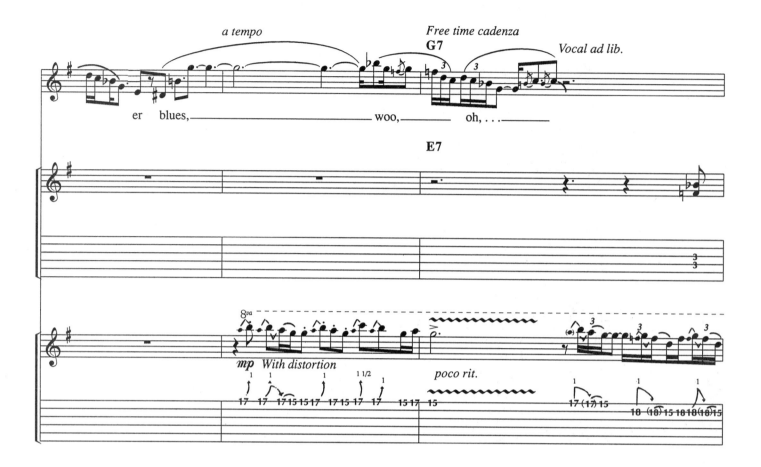

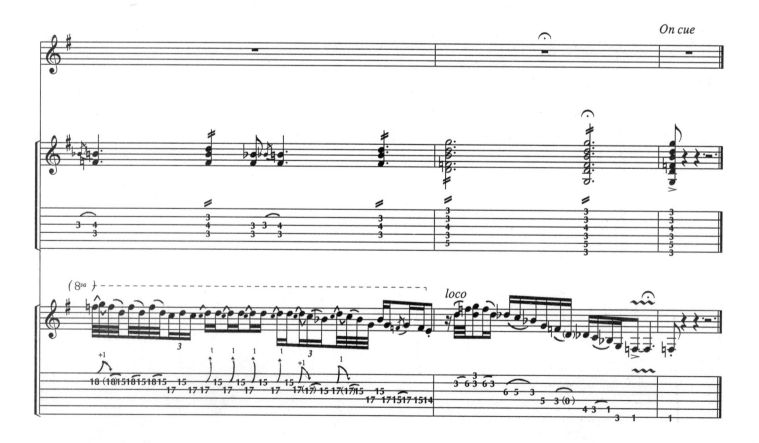